ADOPTION IN IV. CENTURY ATHENS

OPUSCULA GRAECOLATINA
Edenda curavit Ivan Boserup
Vol. 34

Adoption in IV. Century Athens

by

Lene Rubinstein

MUSEUM TUSCULANUM PRESS
University of Copenhagen 1993

© 1993 by Museum Tusculanum Press & Lene Rubinstein
Computer typeset / laserprinted by Lene Rubinstein
Printed in Denmark at Fihl-Jensens Bogtrykkeri, Copenhagen
ISBN 87 7289 204 8
ISSN 0107 8089

Published with the support of
The Carlsberg Foundation

MUSEUM TUSCULANUM PRESS
University of Copenhagen
92 Njalsgade
DK-2300 Copenhagen S

Table of Contents

Preface by *M.H.Hansen and P.A.Cartledge*	vii
Acknowledgements	ix
1. Introduction	1
2. Who adopted and who were adopted?	16
1. Legal requirements	16
2. The individual cases compiled in the catalogue	21
Adoption inter vivos	21
Testamentary adoption	22
Posthumous adoption	25
Adoption and social status	29
3. Procedures of adoption	33
1. The private agreement	34
2. Enrolment in phratry and deme	36
3. Effects of the three procedures of adoption	45
4. Annulment of adoption	55
4. Why did the Athenians adopt?	62
1. γηροτροφία	64
2. The private tomb-cult and Athenian οἶκοι	68
3. Adoption and the order of intestate succession	76
5. Adoption and ἐπίκληροι	87
1. Adoption as a supplement to the ἐπίκληρος-institution	88
2. Adoption as an alternative to the ἐπίκληρος-institution	92
3. Adoption of daughters' sons	97
6. Posthumous adoption and intestate heirs	105
1. Posthumous adoption - a legal obligation?	106
2. Posthumous adoption - a moral obligation?	109
7. Conclusion	113
Catalogue of attested adoptions	117
Stemmata	126
Bibliography	134
Index of sources	141
General index	147

*To M. Toubro
in gratitude*

Preface
by M. H. Hansen and P. A. Cartledge

In 1986 Lene Rubinstein was one of the four graduate students who joined me in setting up *The Copenhagen Nekro-File*, a database recording all Athenian citizens known to have been commemorated in sepulchral inscriptions from ca. 400 B.C. (when it became common to add the demotic to the name and patronymic) to ca. A.D. 250 (when the habit of recording the demotic was discontinued). In addition to building up the base we decided to use the data to shed light on some problems of Athenian demography.

One problem was how the 139 demes managed to survive demographically from ca. 500 B.C. to ca. A.D. 300. Relying on the professional demographers whom we consulted, we at first believed that at least some of the smaller demes, if left to natural population development, would have become extinct over the 750 years from Kleisthenes' reforms to the Herulian sack of Athens. But all the demes seem in fact to have survived into the third century A.D. The simplest explanation in our opinion was adoption, which, if widely practised, must have preserved many families who would otherwise have died out.

It fell to Lene Rubinstein as a member of the group to study Athenian adoption, on the hypothesis that the preservation of all demes was an argument in favour of the importance of that institution in the Classical, Hellenistic, and Roman periods. But we then came across evidence from which it could be inferred that, demographically, there was nothing odd about the survival of all the small demes. Even without resorting to adoption to supplement natural growth any group consisting of 20-30 lineages could easily survive for seven centuries and even more. There was thus no need to suppose that even a small deme was dependent for its survival on adoption (see Hansen et al., "The Demography of the Attic Demes. The Evidence of the Sepulchral Inscriptions" in *Analecta Romana* 19 (1990) 30-32). Accordingly, we had to change horses in midstream.

Lene Rubinstein, however, had already produced such an excellent study of adoption that she continued her studies under my supervision, but detached from the demographic researches based on the Nekro-File, to which she contributed by being the first author of an article on adoption in Hellenistic and Roman Athens. The result of her studies of Athenian adoption in the Classical period was an M.A. thesis of outstanding quality. On the assumption that all Athenian citizens were members of phratries both in the Archaic and Classical periods, she convincingly transplanted the institution of adoption from the private sphere (a contract between adopter and adoptee) to the public sphere (enrolment into the phratry of the adopter). She came up with the first plausible explanation of posthumous adoption and gave a balanced account of the various forms of adoption practised, basing her investigations on a tabulation of all attested adoptions in the Classical period.

M.H.H.

Mogens Herman Hansen advised Lene Rubinstein to revise and expand her M.A. thesis and to turn it into a short monograph in English, and for that purpose she was awarded a scholarship by the Carlsberg Foundation to pursue her research in Cambridge, England, under my supervision. The process of revision and expansion has been carried out in exemplary fashion, but it has led also to several modification of the original thesis, one of which deserves special mention here. According to the generally shared scholarly perception, powerfully supported by a reading of Aristotle's *Politics*, the Greek *polis* was a community in the strong sense that communal interests typically took precedence over individual and private ones. It is therefore also widely assumed by scholars that the *polis* would have taken all necessary measures to maintain as functioning units the *oikoi* (households) that collectively constituted the community. Lene Rubinstein's brilliant study has confounded that assumption with regard to adoption at any rate. The community of Classical Athens did not in fact intervene actively to preserve *oikoi* through adoption, indeed the initiative for preserving *oikoi* was left entirely up to private individuals. Rather than social pressure, it was individual concern for providing a descendant for oneself that constituted the chief motive force behind adoption in classical Athens. This is a major revision of received opinion and will help to guarantee Lene Rubinstein's important monograph a large and eager readership.

P.A.C.

Acknowledgements

Since work on this book, in the shape of a Danish MA-dissertation, began already five years ago at the University of Copenhagen and later travelled with me to Cambridge, the number of people who have offered me help and advice at various stages is indeed vast. I owe my greatest debt of gratitude to my two supervisors at the universities of Copenhagen and Cambridge respectively, Dr. Mogens Herman Hansen and Dr. Paul A. Cartledge. Mogens Herman Hansen supervised my work for two years in Copenhagen and, later, has always been prepared to offer suggestions, criticism, and encouragement, even after I moved to Cambridge. Paul Cartledge adopted the rôle as my supervisor in 1990 and has in this connection patiently read through numerous successive English versions of the text, commenting on almost every possible aspect ranging from method, sources, and Athenian law in general to grammar, spelling, and punctuation. I have been entirely depending on their advice and support, which I have never lacked.

I am also indebted to Prof. John Crook who read the entire original manuscript in Danish, saw me through the first difficult phases of producing an English version, and made numerous comments on its contents. Prof. Theodore Buttrey kindly undertook to revise the manuscript at its final stage. Furthermore, I would like to thank Dr. Paul Millett, Prof. David Konstan, Dr. Karl Hölkeskamp, Dr. Peter Garnsey, Cand.Phil. Thomas Heine Nielsen, friends and fellow-students at the University of Cambridge, and my mother, judge Ulla Rubinstein, who have all read earlier drafts of the book and discussed various chapters and sections with me. They have saved me from many errors, but such errors as remain are entirely my own responsibility.

Thanks are also due to Dr. D.J.Thompson and other fellows and staff at Girton College for having made my stay in Cambridge possible.

Last, but not least, I would like to thank the Carlsberg Foundation for having generously supported this project financially with a publication grant in addition to two successive studentships which allowed me to continue my work on adoption in classical Athens, from April 1990 till this day.

Churchill College *Lene Rubinstein*
September 1992

Chapter 1: Introduction

Adoption in IV.century Athens has not recently been treated in all its aspects in an independent study[1]. It has formed part of more widely defined investigations of Athenian law in general and family law in particular and of the Athenian family-structure, or it has been treated in shorter specialised treatises dealing with particular problems related to the working of the institution. Often, indeed, the institution of adoption is treated merely as a side-issue, for example in works dealing with Athenian funerary customs, where the existence of the institution is seen as testifying to the importance of private tomb-cult in the IV. century; or in connection with studies of the Athenian epiclerate, where the Athenian practice of adoption lends credibility to the assumption that preservation of Athenian οἶκοι had a central place in Athenian thought and legislation[2]. Of course, to study adoption in isolation from its wider social and legal context would lead nowhere. But the aim of the present investigation is to throw light on this institution in particular, so that tomb-cult, as well as aspects of Athenian family-life and the Athenian legislation which regulated it, are treated only in so far as they have a direct bearing on the Athenian institution of adoption.

In Athens, adoption could take place in three different ways. Firstly, the adoption could be carried out while the adopter himself was still alive. This type of adoption is normally referred to as adoption *inter vivos*, and the same terminology will be used in this book. Secondly, a man could nominate an heir in his will, stipulating that his beneficiary was to succeed him as his adopted son (or daughter), socalled testamentary adoption. And, thirdly, if a man died without leaving a legitimate son, whether natural or adopted, a posthumous adoption could be carried out on his behalf without the adopter's having played any active part in the procedure at all. It will be argued in chapter 2 that

---

[1] The latest monograph on adoption is M. Podo (1957) which, unfortunately, was not accessible. Apparently, it has never been reviewed, and it has left no trace in any subsequent treatment of adoption. In 1961, F.Brindesi published a long essay on Athenian adoption in *La famiglia attica. Il matrimonio e l'adozione*.

[2] Adoption plays an important part of Fustel de Coulanges' construction of the Athenian family (1980 ed., pp. 40-48) His views greatly influenced the work of e.g. Beauchet (1897) and Bruck (1909) and (1926), and more indirectly, Lipsius (1905-15) pp. 58, 508sq. and 574sq., Wolff (1944) p.50, 93sqq. and (1978)10sq., Gernet (1955), Jones (1956), Brindesi (1961), and Lacey (1968).

a person was only eligible for posthumous adoption, if he had already been recognised as the intestate heir of the deceased by the People's Court by an inheritance-procedure called ἐπιδικασία (or sometimes διαδικασία if the court was to decide on several contesting claims)[3].

The choice of the institution of adoption as a focus of attention in this work may need further justification. In the detailed juristic treatments of the institution, it has been classified as belonging to the sphere of "private law". Much attention has been devoted e.g. to the contractual nature of the adoption which was carried out *inter vivos* as opposed to the unilateral nature of a testamentary adoption (where a testator would nominate an adoptee in his will); the difference between the two types of adoption is alleged to have been one of substance rather than procedure. In the present work it will be argued that the main difference between the two types of adoption was one of procedure: adoption took place in public, in the adopter's phratry and deme, no matter whether prior to the death of the adopter (as was the case in an adoption *inter vivos*) or posthumously (in the case of testamentary and posthumous adoption). It will be argued, further, that it was the formal recognition of the adoptee by the adopter's phratry and deme which constituted the adoption itself and gave it its validity, legal as well as social. Thus, the distinction between "private" and "public" begins to break down.

On the other hand, an attempt has been made here to break away from a view which has often been stated: that adoption was also a concern of the πόλις, which sought by this means to maintain a constant number of κλῆροι. Consequently, in modern treatises adoption often serves as an illustration of the link between the individual οἶκοι and their superstructure, the πόλις, of which the οἶκος formed the basic unit[4]. It has

---

[3] The term "intestate heir" will be used throughout as denoting a person who had the best claim, by virtue of kinship, to the inheritance left by a childless man. The Athenian order of intestate succession is defined in the (probably incomplete) law-text quoted in [Dem.] XLIII.51 and by the speaker of Isaios XI (11-13). The Athenians recognised as potential heirs both paternal and maternal relatives as far removed as "sons of cousins" (on the ambiguity of this term, see ch.3, n.52). This group of potential heirs was called ἀγχιστεία, and it will be referred to by the Greek term. All paternal relatives within the ἀγχιστεία took precedence over maternal relatives. Males always took precedence over females, so that if a childless man had both a brother and a sister, for example, only his brother would inherit.Children descended from his brother also took precedence over his sister and her children. Relatives who were equally closely related to the deceased would share the inheritance between them: the Athenians did not recognise primogeniture.
[4] As represented by Aristotle in the first book of his *Politika*, e.g. in 1253b. The works of Lacey (1968) and Sissa (1986) may be mentioned as examples of works strongly influenced by *Politika* I; contrast e.g. Hansen (1991, pp.61-5), who prefers to draw on

been debated to what extent exactly the πόλις intervened actively in order to encourage or even force the childless Athenian (or his heirs on his behalf) to perpetuate his family-line. But it is generally agreed that the perpetuation of individual οἶκοι was indeed a concern of the entire community[5]. In the present treatise, however, I have tried to show that, although the Athenians certainly recognised adoption as a legal institution, there is no trace in our sources of any centralised attempt to encourage adoption, by law or otherwise, in the IV. century. On the basis of the arguments employed in lawcourt speeches dealing with inheritance, it will be suggested that the Athenians rather seemed to show a curious lack of interest in the fate of their fellow-citizen's οἶκος. The decision to adopt, it will be argued, rested entirely with the individual Athenian, and what may have been his reasons for making such a decision are discussed in chapter 4.

When describing an institution and how it worked, we may want to decide what would be a "normal" case of an adoption. Those cases which represented clear deviations from the Athenian norm are, of course, also of interest to us, but only if we can decide exactly how they deviated from what was considered "normal" and acceptable. But there is a risk that the very nature of our sources for the working of the institution may render it impossible for us to tell exactly what the Athenians would accept as "normal". We have no epigraphical evidence for adoption in the IV. century, and thus we are effectively barred from drawing conclusions, on a statistical basis, as to what would have been a typical case of adoption[6]. Our most important sources for adoption in the IV. century are lawcourt speeches, and we hear almost nothing about those adoptions that went unchallenged.

When challenging the validity of an adoption, any speaker would try to point out that the adoption under attack deviated in some way or other from the accepted norm. On the other hand, we may expect to find the "model adoption" described in those speeches which were

---

the third book of *Politika*, in which Aristotle works with the *citizen* as the basic unit of the πόλις and not the οἶκος.

[5] Beauchet (1897) may be mentioned as one of the early advocates for this view. Among later scholars of the same opinion are e.g. Lacey (1968), pp.97sqq. and pp.125sqq., Harrison (1968) p.92sq., R.Sealey (1987) p.29, D.Schaps (1979),p.32. See n. 2, above.

[6] M.I.Finley (1952) is an excellent illustration of how a particular category of epigraphical sources may throw light on the working of a legal and social institution when treated, in Finley's own words, as a statistical series.

delivered in defence of adoptions. From this point of view it is of little importance to us whether the adoptions described had actually taken place in the way alleged by the speakers. For even if the speakers are not telling the truth about the adoptions in question, it is safe to assume that the adoptions were presented to the audience in such a way that they would seem both plausible and acceptable. Unfortunately, the number of law-court speeches having a direct bearing on adoption is very limited. Isaios I, IV, V, IX, and X and [Dem.] XLIV all constitute attacks on adoptions, whereas Isaios II, III, VI, and VII were delivered in defence of adoptions. Furthermore, an attempt to describe a "model adoption" is found in [Dem.] XLIII: although it was not the adoption itself that was the main issue of the law-suit, the speaker is basing his case on the validity of a posthumous adoption, and the adoption is described in detail.

I have attempted to balance the generalizations on adoption made in the forensic speeches by compiling the attested Athenian adoptions known to have been carried out in the IV. century. The total number of these is 36, which is obviously too low to form any reasonable basis for statistical calculations. But, taken together, the actual adoptions may still be used to confirm, and in some cases even to undermine, the generalizing statements presented by the speakers in the Athenian lawcourts. The adoptions have been compiled in a catalogue divided into four sections, one for each type of adoption (*inter vivos*, testamentary, and posthumous), and one comprising the adoptions of unknown type. Relevant information pertaining to the circumstances of individual adoptions has been included under each entry.

In addition to the corpus of Athenian forensic oratory, Menander's comedies have been used as evidence, but with even greater caution. Invaluable as they are when used as evidence for Athenian family-life, it is dangerous to use them as evidence for Athenian family-law in direct comparison with information derived from the forensic speeches. It is highly doubtful to what extent we may legitimately deduce from the behaviour of Menander's individual characters any supplementary evidence for provisions in Athenian legislation on the family[7]. Admittedly, the problems which the characters face in the comedies are often centred on legal issues, but when comparing Menander's comedies

---

[7] As has been done e.g. by U.E.Paoli (1961) and D.M.MacDowell (1982).

to the works of the Attic Orators it is essential to be aware of the difference in genre.

Menander's purpose *is* fundamentally different from that of a speaker in an Athenian lawcourt. S.C.Humphreys has made the observation that what is depicted in a forensic speech is the idealised family: the lawcourt is a "theater for the dramatisation of an ideological view of the οἶκος"[8]. Deviations from the ideal will usually be carefully signposted by the speaker, because they serve a specific purpose in his argumentation, that of blackening his opponent[9]. In those cases where a speaker is forced to admit to certain unpleasant facts pertaining to his own conduct or the conduct of his closest kin, the signposting will consist in an attempt to explain and excuse his (or their) abnormal behaviour[10]. But Menander is not out to show an idealised picture of the Athenian family; rather, his aim is to entertain by showing individual conflicts with and reactions to society. Furthermore, we cannot rule out the possibility that some of Menander's humour depends to a certain extent on elements of surprise, that is, on his characters' acting contrary to the immediate expectations of his audience of how an Athenian would "normally" respond to a complex situation.

Therefore, the fact that his comedies are concerned with the emotions of his characters, whereas this aspect is suppressed in the works of the Attic Orators (or sometimes formulated in entirely different terms), is due to a difference in genre rather than to a fundamental change in the Athenians' reactions to their legislation on the family as has often been alleged.

It will be noted that Isokrates XIX (*Aiginetikos*), which deals with a testamentary adoption made by a non-Athenian outside Athens, did not appear among the forensic speeches listed as sources on page 3. In spite of the allegation made by the speaker of Isaios II that "all other people,

---

[8] (1983b) p.9
[9] The examples are legion, but see e.g. Dem.LIX.48 and 64sqq. on Stephanos' and Neaira's behaviour, Isaios III 8-14 on the mother of Phile, Isaios IX.17 on Thoudippos who assaulted and killed his own brother when they were to divide the estate left by their father, Isaios VIII.40-42 on Diokles' having deprived his half-sisters of their right to their inheritance and his subsequent assault on his half-sisters' husbands.
[10] Lysias III.3-4 on the speaker's uncontrollable desire for a young boy, XXXII.11-13 on the speaker's mother-in law denouncing her own father at a family-council, Isaios VI.17-22 on the speaker's father's involvement with an alleged prostitute, which is ascribed to his being senile. Add to this the commonplace of excuse whenever kin ended up as opponents in court.

both Greeks and barbarians, find that this law, the law on adoption, is excellent, and for this reason they all use it"[11], the sources which form the basis of the present investigation are all concerned specifically with the Athenian institution. No attempt has been made, either, to extract information from the papyri or, indeed, any documents which may throw light on adoption as it functioned outside Athens, such as, for example, the laws of Gortyn. The issue of whether we can operate with such a concept as "Greek Law" is highly debatable[12], and when dealing with the Athenian institution of adoption it is particularly dangerous to use information pertaining to adoption in other πόλεις or in Hellenistic Egypt to fill those gaps in our knowledge which our Athenian sources leave open. One reason for this is that the Athenian institution of adoption was inextricably bound up with the concept of Athenian citizenship and the rules pertaining to it, and that the involvement of the demes and the phratries in the procedure constituted the crucial part of an adoption.

We often accept Athenian society as exceptional when dealing with her political institutions; we must beware of the risk that her social institutions, too, may have deviated considerably from what was the case in other Greek πόλεις. We know for a fact, for example, that the position of an Athenian ἐπίκληρος was indeed different from that of a Gortynian πατροιδκος, and that it would be pointless to use the Gortyn Laws as direct supplementary evidence for the working of the Athenian institution. Comparative studies may yield interesting results in their own right for purposes of contrast as much as noting similarities, but *before* undertaking them it will often be to our advantage to throw as much light as possible on each of the institutions we would like to compare.

Often, however, the very nature of our source material renders such comparative studies, perhaps particularly those comparing Athenian legal institutions with those of other Greek πόλεις, extremely difficult, if not impossible. For example, the picture of Gortynian society which we can make up on the basis of the Gortyn Laws is incomplete, and so is our picture of IV. century Athenian society which we may piece together when reading the works of the Attic Orators or Menander. If

---

[11] καὶ τοῖς μὲν ἄλλοις ἅπασιν ἀνθρώποις καὶ Ἕλλησι καὶ βάρβαροις δοκεῖ καλῶς οὗτος ὁ νόμος κεῖσθαι, ὁ περὶ τῆς ποιήσεως, καὶ διὰ τοῦτο χρῶνται πάντες αὐτῷ, II.24.
[12] For a recent contribution to this debate and an overview of the research conducted within the field of Greek legal history, see Todd and Millett (1990).

we want to compare the two, our task is complicated by the fact that the two pictures are incomplete in two different ways. We have no Athenian parallel to the collection (not, strictly, a "code") of the Gortyn Laws to work from, and we have no Gortynian parallel to the arguments presented in an Athenian forensic speech which are based on appeals to unwritten norms and moral values as much as on references to Athenian laws. It is highly questionable to what extent we may compare (and contrast) our relatively scanty data on Athenian written laws to the evidence from the Gortyn inscriptions, just as it would be dangerous to draw conclusions regarding the current Gortynian *interpretation* and *application* of their laws on the basis of moral values and norms expressed in Athenian forensic oratory. In the main body of the present work, no attempt has been made to compare the Athenian institution to adoption elsewhere, although I am aware of the risk that, in the words of S.Todd and P.Millett, "historians who reject the explicit use of comparative evidence tend to use it implicitly and subconsciously"[13].

There is an additional reason why evidence from the papyri has not been included in this investigation. Scholars have compared the Athenian social institutions to the institutions which we find described in the papyri from Hellenistic Egypt, mostly assuming the existence of a universal Greek law. Very often, the explanation offered for the lack of certain social or legal institutions in Hellenistic Egypt, or the differences between Athenian and Hellenistic-Egyptian institutions is chronological: the institutions we find in Hellenistic Egypt represent a further (i.e. later) development of the institutions that were found in classical Greece (and because of the nature of our sources this usually means classical *Athens*). The disappearance or modification of certain institutions, as, for example, that of the ἐπίκληρος, is ascribed to the alleged disintegration of the Greek πόλις, which was replaced by Hellenistic monarchy. It has been argued that with the disintegration of the πόλις-community a new, more individualistic era began, which caused some fundamental changes in the traditional family-structure, the cornerstone of the classical Greek πόλις.

This view can be traced back to the beginning of this century. E.F.Bruck is one of the important exponents of the hypothesis that the institution of adoption underwent a change towards secularisation during the IV. century, both in his *Die Schenkung auf den Todesfall im*

---

[13] Todd and Millett (1990),p.6.

griechischen und römischen Recht, and notably in *Totenteil und Seelgerät im griechischen Recht*. Here he ascribes the change of the legal and social institution to fundamental ideological and religious changes in society which allegedly took place in the late classical and early Hellenistic era[14]. Lipsius, in spite of his generally synchronic approach in *Das attische Recht und Rechtsverfahren*, also assumes that the IV. century was a phase of transition[15]. Gernet, part of whose programme was to investigate the "stratigraphy" of Attic law[16], suggests that the concept of "inheritance" became increasingly materialistic during the IV. century, and he ties up this development with a shift in emphasis from collectivism to individualism in the same period[17].

Harrison's *The Law of Athens* has had a considerable influence on scholars who work within the Anglo-Saxon tradition, and it is still often used as the book of reference in treatises that deal with the Athenian family without taking a particular interest in the strictly legal aspects of adoption[18]. Although Harrison states in his preface that the scope of his inquiry is restricted to the IV. century, a tacit assumption underlying his interpretation of the sources, especially for posthumous adoption, is that the IV. century was a period of economic and ideological change[19]. And in his chapter on wills he apologises for omitting to discuss the evolution of the Athenian will, since "it is particularly true of this topic that the period [of the Orators] was one of transition and that the rules then prevailing can only be fully understood in the light of the evolution as a whole"[20].

Claude Mossé and E.Karabélias may be counted among the more recent exponents of the assumption that the IV. century was a phase of transition in which the archaic and classical set of values in regard to the family was breaking down. Both of them have made numerous and

---

[14] (1926), see esp. his conclusion of III. Buch, pp.271-276.
[15] (1905-15), pp.561-4.
[16] This is expressed clearly in Gernet (1955), p. 85.
[17] Gernet (1955), pp.147sqq.
[18] E.g. by R.Just (1989) and M.Golden (1990), p.137 n. 93, where Harrison is referred to as an authority on posthumous adoption. The section on adoption and wills in MacDowell (1978), pp.99-101 is much influenced by Harrison's conclusions, as is indeed his entire chapter on the family (pp.84-108).
[19] E.g. p.93 "Pressure of economic circumstances in the fourth century was making it more and more difficult to meet these requirements [the ideal that one οἶκος=one κλῆρος] and at the same time keep the rules clear. Posthumous adoption was a rather clumsy device for perpetuating οἶκοι, and the Hagnias and Archiades cases show how uncertain the rules were."
[20] p.149.

important contributions to the study of Athenian family law. The underlying trend of their work is to point out internal inconsistencies in the Athenian attitude to the family as expressed in the works of the Attic Orators and Menander's comedies. Both scholars ascribe these inconsistencies to a drastic change in Athenian ideology partly caused by a change in the economic structure of the Athenian πόλις[21]. When treating the further development of the family in the Hellenistic era, they point to the disintegration of the classical Greek πόλις which allegedly left the classical concept of the family as a collective organism in an ideological vacuum[22].

Now, there is ample evidence that Athens continued to function internally as a πόλις even after the Macedonian conquest. Here it must suffice for the purpose of illustration to recall that the possibilities of acquiring Athenian citizenship were still restricted right up to ca. 140 B.C., the date of our latest known citizenship-decree[23]. Citizenship, up to that date, depended first and foremost on having been born an Athenian, and in that respect, at least, little had changed since the classical era. We need further internal evidence to prove that the Athenian family-structure did actually change during the late IV. century and the Hellenistic period before relying on the papyri as evidence. To point to similar, yet different institutions in Hellenistic Egypt in order to prove that a change had indeed taken place seems from a logical point of view to be begging the question.

For the institution of adoption there is in fact epigraphical evidence which shows that the Athenians continued to practise adoption at least until the II. century A.D. Whether the institution had changed drastically or had at least been modified in the course of the six centuries is impossible to tell, and, again, part of the reason is that the two types of evidence, the IV. century Athenian forensic speeches and

---

[21] E. Karabélias (1975), (1982), C. Mossé (1989a), (1989b). See also A.French (1991), p.27. R.F.Wevers (1969) argues that the general picture which emerges from the speeches of Isaios is that of a society in decay (p.121), and he interprets the large number of adoptions as evidence for a "trend towards childlessness" and for the wealthy IV. century Athenians' committing "race suicide" (p.115). Although Wevers' view is more extreme than that of most other scholars dealing with IV. century Athens, there still is a general tendency to regard the IV. century as a phase of transition, during which society as a whole was secularised and moved towards the rational.
[22] See e.g. E. Karabélias (1982), pp.223-234.
[23] See M. Osborne (1981-83) vol. III-IV, p.144. Davies (1977) holds that the descent-group criterion underwent a certain erosion during the third century, but that it was only redefined in the mid-second century.

the inscriptions which inform us exclusively of the institution in the period from the II. century B.C. onwards are hardly comparable. But the view that the importance of the institution was declining during the IV. century and the early Hellenistic era is hard to maintain without additional evidence.

Traditionally, much attention has been devoted to the history of the institution of adoption, and, therefore, the synchronic approach of this account may need some further justification. The law that is always quoted, paraphrased, and referred to as the law warranting adoption in the forensic speeches is the law passed by Solon, which conferred on the Athenians the right of disposing legally of one's property (διατίθεσθαι τὰ ἑαυτοῦ)[24]. The quotation from Harrison's *The Law of Athens* above illustrates this trend in modern scholarship: it is generally perceived as impossible to understand the institution of adoption as it worked in the IV. century without considering the history of the institution.

Accordingly, many scholars have been preoccupied with determining what Solon intended by passing this law and how the law slotted into his wider programme of social and economic reform[25]. In the present work, however, I have chosen not to join the debate, and I shall state the reasons for my decision here.

The first is that the debate on what was the real purpose of the law is largely based on the axiom that the rôle of the archaic lawgiver was one of innovation. "Solon innove" is the frank statement of Gernet in "La loi de Solon sur le «testament»" and his primary goal in this article is to determine what was the actual innovation[26]. But it may indeed be debated whether it is permissible to work with such an axiom. In his article "'διατίθεσθαι τὰ ἑαυτοῦ'. Ein Beitrag zum sogenannten Testamentsgesetzt des Solon", Ruschenbusch has suggested that, in passing his law on τὸ διατίθεσθαι τὰ ἑαυτοῦ, Solon did nothing but regulate a practice that already existed, in an attempt to meet those controversies and problems, which usually arose in connection with

---

[24] The law is quoted in full in [Dem.] XLVI.14.
[25] See Gernet (1955), pp. 122sq. for references to the pre-1920 debate. Of post-1920 contributions the following may be mentioned: E. Ruschenbusch (1962), D. Asheri (1963), , W.K. Lacey (1968), pp.88sqq., G.E.M. de Sainte Croix (1970), R. Lane Fox (1985), pp. 224sq.
[26] (1955)p.142.

bequest. This is a plausible interpretation, but to investigate further the rôle of Solon as a lawgiver is outside the scope of this work[27].

The second reason is that Solon's intentions with passing his law may only be determined when seen in the light of the social and economic conditions prevailing in the VI. century B.C. Again, one of my reasons for not entering this debate is one of simple economy. Traditionally, Solon's law has been seen as an innovation in that it recognised and liberated the individual from the dominance of the *genos*, conferring on him the right to choose an heir and pass on his property to him. Now, the issue of the archaic *gene* and their rôle in the archaic period is a matter of deep controversy. In 1976 Bourriot published his important book *Recherches sur la nature du Génos. Étude d'histoire sociale athénienne*, in which he questioned the orthodox view of this social institution in the archaic period; and the debate goes on. But economic considerations is not my only reason for not entering this debate, and this brings me to the third and most important argument in my defence of a synchronic approach.

Our most important sources for the pre-IV. century development are, in fact, the works of the IV. century Attic Orators supplemented with Solon's actual law-text quoted in [Dem.] XLVI.14 and Plutarch's Solon-biography. Gernet, for example, worked with the hypothesis that the development of certain legal institutions could be determined by means of an analysis of the IV.century forensic speeches, for, as he said, "dans le droit athénien du IVe siècle, il y a nécessairement une stratification, et nous devons nous attendre à des survivances ou à des archaismes"[28]. Now, I do not claim that the institution of adoption did remain unchanged over the nine centuries in which we know that the Athenians practised adoption[29]. But I will maintain that it is indeed questionable to what extent we may regard the corpus of Athenian forensic oratory as an archaeological trench.

When trying to reconstruct the history of the institution of adoption, it is necessary to build almost exclusively on an interpretation of the

---

[27] See also Boncompto (1954). I am grateful to Dr. Karl J. Hölkeskamp for having spent time discussing this issue with me after his very inspiring paper delivered in The Cambridge Philological Society, spring 1991.
[28] (1955), p.85.
[29] The latest known Athenian adoptions are attested in IG II.2 2930 and 9735 dated to the II. or III. century A.D. The retrospective clause in Solon's law, ὅσοι μὴ ἐπεποίηντο... testifies to the fact that adoptions were carried out at least as early as the VI. century.

works of the Attic Orators. However, it is inevitable that the interpretation itself will be affected by the interpreter's preconceived idea of the direction in which the institution moved. In the diachronic analyses of Athenian adoption there is a marked desire to see the archaic period as "the other" and to contrast this with the "modern" and "individualistic" Hellenistic age, that is, the age in which the Athenians came to resemble *us*. The IV. century, in this context, is then construed as the phase in which two Athenian sets of values (archaic, religious and collectivistic vs. "modern", secular and individualistic) clashed.

When trying to determine the exact nature of the conflict on the basis of arguments presented in the forensic speeches, Gernet, for example, worked on the assumption that, ideally, the Athenian legal system in the IV. century was *rational* and, logically, internally consistent. In those cases where it was not, he offered a chronological explanation, as in his article "La diamartyrie procédure archaique du droit athénien". Here, as in "La loi de Solon sur le «testament»", one of his means of determining the stratigraphy of Athenian legislation is to point to the judges' negative reaction to a given procedure, as alleged by the speakers in the Athenian courts. In the case of διαμαρτυρία, he argues that the claim made in Isaios VII.3, that the judges are known to frown upon the employment of this procedure, testifies to its archaic nature[30]. In the case of testamentary adoption, the fact that it is "encore considerée au IVe siecle avec un défaveur visible" is interpreted as testifying to the novelty of the institution[31], which had been developed secondarily as a variant of the original (archaic) adoption *inter vivos*.

In both cases, his interpretation of the speakers' allegations is determined by his preconceived idea of what was likely to be archaic survivals, and what was in keeping with IV. century "rational" legislation, and I hope to have illustrated with these two examples that such an approach is indeed questionable from a methodological point of view.

---

[30] (1955), p.85. Gernet does not consider whether the argument of the speaker may belong to the customary set of compliments to the judges ("I do not wish to avoid your (just) judgment", cf. e.g. Antiphon V.8). It does, in fact, fit this category very well, and it is placed in the prooimion of the speech where we would expect to find an argument of this type. Nor does he consider the fact that this particular speaker may have had good reasons not to run the risk connnected with a διαμαρτυρία (see below, chapter 3, sect.3), but that he did not want to be too explicit about them.
[31] (1955), pp.122sq.

Now, Athenian adoption differed fundamentally from the institution of adoption in a modern, western society. We tend to think of adoption as an institution primarily intended for the benefit of the adoptee, that is, usually, a child in need of parental care. For example, the second provision of the Danish law on adoption runs as follows: "The permission to adopt may be granted only if the adoption is considered, on the basis of prior investigation, to be of benefit (4) to the person whom one wishes to adopt, and if the adopter either wishes to bring up the adoptee in the adopter's home or if the adoptee has been brought up [as a foster child] in the adopter's home...". Footnote 4 states that the provision that the adoption must be of benefit to the adoptee "is the main condition of adoption."[32] Not so in Athens. There, the institution was primarily construed as benefitting the adopter, providing for his need of a descendant. In those cases where we know the age of the adoptees, they tend to be adults, as pointed out in chapter 2. This major difference between our institution and that of the Athenians has of course been noted by modern scholars, and the next step is to find out why "having a descendant" was seen as essential by those Athenians who practised adoption. Two answers present themselves in the works of the Orators: one is the need to be provided for in one's old age (γηροτροφία), another to provide for the continuation of one's family-line.

The first is immediately intelligible to the modern reader. Of course, in a social welfare society, the care of the elderly is often conceived of as the responsibility of the state, but one need not travel further than to the Arab countries on the south coast of the Mediterranean to encounter societies where the elderly are entirely dependent on their descendants and other close relatives for material and emotional support. But the second, that of the preservation of family-lines, deviates from our modern set of values and expectations. It is tied up with religion as much as with a conceptualisation of the family which is alien to us.

In this respect, it is worth noting that the aspect of γηροτροφία played a significant rôle as a motivation only in connection with one of the three types of Athenian adoption, namely adoption *inter vivos* as pointed out in chapter 4. Both testamentary and posthumous adoption came into effect only after the death of the adopter, and, as will been noted in

---

[32] Consolidate Act 1986-09-15 no. 629. The Law on Adoption as modified by L 1989-04-05 no. 209 and L 1989-06-07 no. 189, §2. I am grateful to judge Ulla Rubinstein, for having provided me with information pertaining to current Danish legislation on adoption and inheritance.

chapter 2, most of the attested testators were probably young or middle-aged. Thus, the decision to adopt by will or posthumously depended entirely on the adopter's or his heirs' wish to see his family-line continued for another generation.

This may well be the reason why scholars have found it least difficult to accept that the Athenians continued to practise adoption *inter vivos* beyond the close of the IV. century. Here Bruck may be quoted as an example: "Dies hindert natürlich nicht, daß im hellenistischen Zeitalter - *genau so wie heut* - noch Adoptionen unter Lebenden vorkamen, wenn der Kinderlosen das *allgemein menschliche* bedürfnis empfand, ein Kind zu haben" (my italics).[33] Contrarywise, attempts have been made to prove that, in the IV. century, the institutions of posthumous and testamentary adoption were in decline, heralding the beginning of the Hellenistic era.

However, there is ample evidence that the Athenians practised testamentary adoption in the IV. century, and this in turn compels the evolutionists to assume that, in this period, adoption was compulsory when drawing up a will. The fact that bequest was still combined with adoption is seen as a concession to tradition, a survival from an earlier (archaic) age: testamentary *adoption* was not the choice of the individual, but, rather, the inevitable result of drawing up a will with the intention of disrupting the order of intestate succession[34]. Consequently, scholars have done their best to explain away those sources that testify to IV. century wills *not* providing for adoption, on the assumption that adoption was indeed a legal requirement in the age of the Orators.

It will be argued in chapter 4 that this was not the case, and that, accordingly, the attested testamentary adoptions testify to the individual Athenian's desire to see his family-line continued. This is in keeping with the argument in e.g. S.C. Humphreys' important article "Family tombs and tomb cult in Ancient Athens" that Athenian private tomb cult *grew* in importance in the V. and IV. century. From this position, it

---

[33] (1926), p.276.
[34] This view has already been questioned by Hardcastle (1980) and by W.E.Thompson (1981). In both articles J.W. Jones is the main target: in his *The Law and Legal Theory of the Greeks* he advocates the view that, in the IV. century, the Athenian attitude to wills was purely instrumental. Jones has gone even further than the other evolutionists in assuming that the development towards the secularised will had already been completed in the age of the orators, and that the arguments centred on tomb-cult in the forensic speeches were no longer founded in IV. century reality outside the court.

could just as well be argued that wills providing for adoption only came into real prominence in the IV. century, but the source material warrants this conclusion no more (and, in my opinion, no less) than it warrants the traditional theory of evolution.

The present work aims at presenting a coherent picture of how the institution of adoption worked in the IV. century B.C. (but not necessarily a picture of an institution that was logically consistent in the same way as we would expect it from a modern western legal institution). Consequently, no attempt has been made to resolve conflicting statements made in the IV. century forensic speeches by means of chronology. Nor have I detected any sign in the forensic speeches of evolution of the institution in the course of the IV. century, so I have resolved to treat all speeches as if they were contemporary, although, in reality, they span the greater part of a century. The working hypothesis underlying this book is that when doing research in the field of Athenian family-law, we are operating in an area where continuity is to be expected, rather than fundamental change.

Chapter 2: Who adopted and who were adopted?

Who were the parties involved in an adoption? The question will be dealt with in two separate sections in this chapter. In the first the legal requirements will be examined; in the second, an attempt will be made to characterise the inviduals who are known from our sources as either adopters or adoptees. The latter investigation will be based on the evidence compiled in the catalogue. Each type of adoption will be treated separately in the second section of this chapter, because the choice of an adopted son appears to have been bound up with the procedure employed.

1. Legal requirements

Only adult males had the right to adopt. The fact that women and children were not allowed to dispose legally of property worth more than one medimnos of barley meant that they did not have the right to choose an heir to be adopted. This, at least, is what is claimed by the speaker in Isaios X.10[1]. But not all adult males were allowed to adopt: in the Solonic law on wills which is quoted in [Dem.] XLVI.14, the right is limited in the following way:
"It shall be possible for all those, who had not been adopted with the result that they may neither renounce [the inheritance left by the adoptee], nor have to assert their rights in an ἐπιδικασία, when Solon entered his term of office, to dispose of their property as they wish, if they do not have legitimate male children, and if not deranged because of madness, old age, drugs, illness or a woman's persuasion, or compelled by force or imprisonment". ("Οσοι μὴ ἐπεποίηντο, ὥστε μήτε ἀπειπεῖν μήτ' ἐπιδικάσασθαι, ὅτε Σόλων εἰσῄει εἰς τὴν ἀρχήν, τὰ ἑαυτοῦ διαθέσθαι εἶναι ὅπως ἂν ἐθέλῃ, ἂν μὴ παῖδες ὦσι γνήσιοι ἄρρενες, ἂν μὴ

---

[1] ὁ γὰρ νόμος διαρρήδην κωλύει παιδὶ μὴ ἐξεῖναι συμβάλλειν μηδὲ γυναικὶ πέρα μεδίμνου κριθῶν. The speaker is clearly arguing *a fortiori*. That Athenian women were not allowed to adopt is further corroborated by the observation made by Schaps (1979), p.68 on Isaios VII.25.

μανιῶν ἢ γήρως ἢ φαρμάκων ἢ νόσου ἕνεκα, ἢ γυναικὶ πειθόμενος, ὑπὸ τούτων του παρανοῶν, ἢ ὑπ' ἀνάγκης ἢ ὑπὸ δεσμοῦ καταληφθείς.)

It has been debated whether this law was intended to confer the right of drawing up a will on the Athenians, or whether it was a law which allowed the institution of an heir by means of adoption *inter vivos*. But no matter what Solon intended when passing his law in the VI. century, it is quite clear that, in the IV. century, the restrictions enumerated in the law applied to those who adopted *inter vivos* as well as to testators. In Isaios II, which is a speech delivered in defence of an adoption *inter vivos*, the speaker refers to the law[2], and it may be inferred from the argument of the speech as a whole that the opponents based their case on the provision in the law which forbade a man to διατίθεσθαι τὰ ἑαυτοῦ as he wished, if he was under a woman's influence[3]. The institution of an heir by means of adoption *inter vivos* could be conceived of as one way of "disposing of one's property", and the fact that the law is appealed to in the lawcourt speeches as the law permitting adoption *inter vivos* indicates that there was no other law which warranted this procedure in particular[4]. The law required a man to be of sound mind and free from pressure when making such dispositions, and it aimed at ensuring that he did not deprive his legitimate sons of their inheritance. The right to dispose freely of one's property was restricted to those men who had no legitimate, natural sons.

On the other hand, a man would not be legally prevented from adopting an heir if he had only a daughter. It is generally assumed that the adopted son would be required to marry her[5], and the sources inform us of one adoption that was carried out by a man who had two legitimate daughters[6]. A man who was an adopted son himself was not allowed to adopt. In [Dem.] XLIV.68 it is claimed that this provision aimed at ensuring that the inheritance would return to the adopter's relatives if the adopted son did not succeed in continuing the οἶκος of his adoptive father by leaving a son from his own body. It has been debated

---

[2] Isaios II.13.
[3] Isaios II.1, 19, 25, 38.
[4] Ruschenbusch (1957) has argued (*ZGR*, pp.368sq.) that the law on wills was applied to adoption *inter vivos*, simply because there was no written legislation establishing the right to employ the latter procedure (this is what he calls a "Rechtslücke").
[5] Isaios III.48, 68sq., X.13. See e.g. Hruza (1892), pp.118sqq. ,Harrison (1968), pp.85sq , Schaps (1979), p.31. MacDowell (1982) argues that it was possible for a man with a daughter to adopt without marrying her to the adoptee. This will be discussed below in chapter 5.
[6] Cat.no.2.

whether all adoptees were barred from disposing freely of the property of their adoptive fathers by will and/or adoption[7]. But in [Dem.] XLIV.68, where the speaker refers to the provision in the Solonic law, there is no hint that the rule applied only to certain categories of adopted sons. In [Dem.] XLVI.15 the rule is even applied to naturalized citizens who were said metaphorically to have been "adopted by the Athenian people". Even if we have to take the latter interpretation of the law with a grain of salt, it is quite clear that the Athenians in the IV. century would think of the rule as barring any adoptee from adopting, regardless of the procedure by which he had been adopted[8]. A further restriction on the right to adopt is found in Aischines III.21 where we are told that a magistrate who had not yet undergone his εὔθυναι did not have the right to dispose freely of his property.

While we know of a number of legal provisions restricting the right to adopt, almost no legal requirements concerning the right to be adopted have been handed down to us in our sources. But we do know that an adopted son would have to meet the requirements for Athenian citizenship, and for the IV. century it is stated, e.g. in *Ath. Pol.* 42.1, that a man would be entitled to Athenian citizenship only if both his parents were Athenians. In the period with which we are concerned, an adopted son would undoubtedly be expected to meet this requirement of descent, since the rules were strictly enforced in the IV. century[9]. The adopted son became a member of his adoptive father's deme and would exercise his rights as an Athenian citizen as a member of that group. Although it has long been disputed whether all Athenian citizens were

---

[7] See Harrison (1968), pp.85sq. for references to the discussion.

[8] Harrison suggested (*ibid.*, pp.86sq.) that the law only applied to those adopted sons who had not claimed the inheritance of their adoptive father by means of the procedure of adjudication of an inheritance, the ἐπιδικασία, but had exercised their right of ἐμβάτευσις, that is immediate entry on the estate. He infers this from the clause ὥστε μήτε ἀπειπεῖν μήτ' ἐπιδικάσασθαι. But, considering the retrospective context of the provision (ὅσοι μὴ ἐπεποίηντο...), this clause may in fact only have served to state in precise terms the effects of the pre-Solonic adoption, which were, in that case, exactly the same as those of a completed adoption in the IV. century. It will be argued in chapter 3 that, once the adoption had been recognised formally by the adopter's phratry and deme, the adoptee had the right of barring subsequent attempts to instigate ἐπιδικασίαι, and, once adopted, he could not renounce the adoption (ἀπειπεῖν) in order to return to the οἶκος of his natural father, unless he left a legitimate son who would take over the title of adoptee. The right to bar ἐπιδικασίαι and the obligation to remain in the adopter's οἶκος applied to all adopted sons, once the adoption had been completed, regardless of whether the adoptee had been appointed *inter vivos*, by will, or posthumously.

[9] See e.g. Hansen (1991), pp.94sqq.

members of phratries, the tendency recently has been to assume that they were[10]. Membership of an Athenian phratry was conditional not only upon the candidate's parents being citizens, but also on the candidate's having been born in wedlock.

In the following chapter it will be demonstrated that enrolment of the adopted son in his adoptive father's phratry formed a crucial part of the procedure of adoption. In connection with the introduction of a candidate to the phratry of his adoptive father, an oath had to be sworn by the introducer that the candidate had been born from a lawfully married citizen-woman, just as if he had been a natural son.

It was probably not permitted to adopt a person who had lost his rights to exercise his privileges as an Athenian citizen, that is, a person who was an ἄτιμος. Admittedly, there is no piece of evidence which unambiguously confirms that it was illegal, but there are strong indications that this was the case. The verdict passed upon Antiphon and Archeptolemos in 411/10 took the form of a decree which is quoted in [Plut.] *Vit.X Orat*.834b. The two men were sentenced to hereditary ἀτιμία (along with a number of other punishments), and it is stated in the decree that any person found guilty of adopting any of their descendants was himself to be punished with ἀτιμία. At first sight, this would seem to conflict with the statement made in Isaios X.17: "Otherwise people get their children adopted into other οἶκοι, when they are unlucky in financial matters, so that the children will not have to share in their father's ἀτιμία". (ἢ ἕτεροι μὲν, ὅταν περὶ χρημάτων δυστυχῶσιν, τοὺς σφετέρους αὑτοὺς παῖδας εἰς ἑτέρους οἴκους εἰσποιοῦσιν, ἵνα μὴ μετάσχωσι τῆς τοῦ πατρὸς ἀτιμίας). Harrison argued that the ban on adoption in the case of Antiphon and Archeptolemos was a special provision which applied to the descendants of these two men only[11]. He interprets the fact that the provision was mentioned in the decree at all as an indication that it was not general, but exceptional.

His argument may be countered, however, by referring to the Athenian convention of including general provisions in their decrees, notably those conferring citizenship on individuals. In each case it is stated that the candidate is to get himself enrolled in a phratry and a

---

[10] E.g. Hansen (1986), appendix 2, pp.73-76, Sissa (1986) pp.170sqq., Patterson (1981), (1990), Hedrick (1990), p.vii, (1991) p.250.
[11] (1968), p.89.

deme[12], and although this provision seems to have been general, the Athenians took the trouble to inscribe it on each individual decree. This attested practice removes at least part of the foundation of Harrison's argument. Furthermore, in his *Apagoge, Endeixis, and Ephegesis against Kakourgoi, Atimoi, and Pheugontes*, Hansen has demonstrated that the statements made in the two sources are easily reconciled and explained by the fact that hereditary ἀτιμία could affect the descendants of the convicts in two different ways[13]. In the Isaios passage quoted above, the speaker is referring to those men who had incurred hereditary ἀτιμία as state-debtors. The descendants of a state-debtor would incur ἀτιμία only when they inherited the debt of their father at the latter's death. Until then they were ἐπίτιμοι, and, if they were adopted before the death of their father, they would avoid inheriting both his debt and his loss of citizen-rights. Antiphon and Archeptolemos, on the other hand, had been convicted of treason, and the punishment of this crime included ἀτιμία which instantly hit the descendants of the convict. There was no time-span between the pronouncement of the verdict and its imposition on the descendants in which they were ἐπίτιμοι and thus eligible for adoption by another citizen. In short, the provision included in the verdict passed on Antiphon and Archeptolemos indicates that it was forbidden to adopt an ἄτιμος, and that violation of this rule was to be punished with ἀτιμία. A further restriction on the right to be adopted applied to the magistrates: just as they were not allowed to adopt, so they could not themselves be adopted, before having undergone their εὔθυναι[14].

There was, apparently, no legal requirement as to the age of the adoptee, nor was the right to be adopted restricted to male Athenians. We know three female adoptees from the IV. century sources[15], namely Apollodoros' uterine half-sister whom Apollodoros named as his beneficiary in his will[16], Hagnias' niece[17], and the daughter of Theophon's sister[18]. In all three cases the circumstances of these

---

[12] See M.Osborne (1981-83), checklist in vol.I pp.17-24, categories I-XIV, and generally on formulae in citizenship decrees in vol.IV pp.155-170.
[13] pp.71sq.
[14] Aisch. III.21.
[15] More examples of adoption of Athenian women are found in the epigraphical sources, IG II 2.3520; 3909; 4720-22; 6482; 9949; 9735 , but these are all later than II. century B.C. and will not be considered here.
[16] Isaios VII.9, cat. no.9.
[17] Isaios XI.8sq., cat. no.13.
[18] Isaios XI.41, 45, cat. no.17.

adoptions are not explained in any detail, but it must be assumed that a female adoptee would have had to meet the same requirements on descent from married citizen-parents as would an adopted son.

2. The individual cases compiled in the catalogue

Adoption inter vivos

We know of only five examples of adoption *inter vivos*, and it will therefore be impossible to draw general conclusions with any certainty on the basis of this material. But there are facts in each individual case which seem to point in the same direction: of the five adopters four were married or had been married at some point before adopting *inter vivos*, namely Apollodoros whose inheritance is disputed in Isaios VII[19], Polyeuktos[20] who adopted his brother-in-law, Isokrates who adopted a son born to his wife in a previous marriage[21], and Menekles who adopted the brother of his ex-wife[22]. Only Archiades, known from [Dem.] XLIV, is said to have died a bachelor[23]. It appears that three of the adopters had abandoned hope of begetting natural sons when they carried out their adoptions. Although Menekles had been married twice he had not succeeded in producing any off-spring, while Apollodoros' only son had died not long before Apollodoros' adoption of his nephew, Thrasyllos. Apollodoros, we are informed in Isaios VII.14, adopted "in despair of his present circumstances, cussing his old age" (ἐπὶ τοῖς παροῦσιν ἀθυμήσας καὶ τὴν ἡλικίαν τὴν ἑαυτοῦ καταμεμψάμενος), and Menekles, allegedly, divorced his second wife because he did not want her to grow old and childless with him.[24] Polyeuktos had two daughters and very likely did not expect to have any more children, since he married his youngest daughter to his adopted son, Leokrates, in connection with the adoption. Presumably, at least 14 years had lapsed between the birth of this daughter and the adoption[25].

---

[19] Cat. no.4.
[20] Cat. no.2. Polyeuktos' wife survived him, Dem.XLI.9 and 20sqq.
[21] Cat. no.5 [Plut.] *Vit. X Orat.* 838A.
[22] Cat. no.3, Isaios II.3-4,11.
[23] Cat. no.1. For Archiades' having died a batchelor, see [Dem.] XLIV.18.
[24] Isaios II.7.
[25] See e.g. S.Isager (1982) p.86 for a discussion of the marriageable age of Athenian women.

As for the relationship between the adopters and adoptees Gernet has shown on the evidence available that adoptive fathers tended to choose their adopted sons from within their ἀγχιστεία[26]. His observation seems to be corroborated by a passage from Isaios II where the speaker is at pains to demonstrate that it was impossible for Menekles to find a candidate for adoption among the persons belonging to his own family-circle[27]. It may therefore be due to pure coincidence that three of the five adoptees adopted *inter vivos* were in fact not members of the ἀγχιστεῖαι of the adopters. And the two adoptees who *were* related to their adoptive fathers by blood, Apollodoros' Thrasyllos and Archiades' Leokrates, both ranked rather low in the order of intestate succession. Since Thrasyllos was the son of Apollodoros' half-sister, all the relatives of Apollodoros on his father's side including the sons of his cousins had a better claim to the inheritance than did Thrasyllos himself, had it not been for his adoption[28]. Leokrates was placed slightly higher up, being the son of the daughter of Archiades' sister[29].

In those cases where we have any information concerning the age of the adoptees at the time of their adoptions, they were adults. Menekles' adopted son had served as a soldier prior to his adoption[30], Thrasyllos had been a thesmothete[31], and Leokrates, who married his adoptive sister, must have been an adult as well. On the other hand, in Menander's *Samia* (695-699) Moschion has been adopted by Demeas while still a little boy, and this probably shows that adoption *inter vivos* of minors was not inconceivable to Menander's audience.

Although the five known examples of adoption *inter vivos* do not allow us to draw any conclusions as to who would "typically" employ this procedure, it is important to note that four out of the five adopters were or had been married before adopting, and that they seem to have reached a relatively advanced age at the time of the adoption.

Testamentary adoption
Although we know twelve examples of testamentary adoption, that is, about twice as many as we do of adoptions performed *inter vivos*, this

---

[26] (1955), pp.129sqq.
[27] Isaios II.21-23.
[28] Isaios VII.7 and 9.
[29] [Dem.] XLIV.17.
[30] Isaios II.6.
[31] Isaios VII.34.

number is still too low to form the basis of any reliable general conclusions. But, again, there are certain characteristics, which the known testators have in common, and these may turn out to be of some significance.

Of the ten known testators six died in war or while travelling[32]. Of the remaining four, Apollodoros drew up his will just before he joined in a military campaign, and after having returned safe and sound he had a natural son born to him[33]. He probably revoked his will at that point[34]. In any case, according to the speaker of Isaios VII, the will must have come out of operation at some stage, since the speaker claims to have been adopted *inter vivos* by Apollodoros. Kleonymos died from illness[35], and for the last two testators we are not informed of the cause of their death. Two of the testators are claimed to have been married: Pyrrhos whose marriage is disputed by the speaker of Isaios III[36], and Philoktemon[37]. Marriage is not mentioned at all in connection with the other testators.

No information is given on the age of the testators; but since we know that some of them had died in war, it is a reasonable assumption that they were less than 59 years old when they had drawn up their wills[38].

As for the adopted heirs, eight of them belonged to the ἀγχιστεῖαι of their adoptive fathers. Four of the adoptees were sisters' sons or daughters, two were sons of cousins, and two were uterine half-siblings of the testators[39]. Moreover, only two of the twelve beneficiaries can be

---

[32] Cat. nos. 8 (war, Isaios V.6), 10 (war, Isaios X.22), 11 (war, Isaios IV.7, 18sq.), 13 (travelling, Isaios XI.8), 14 (war, Isaios IX.15), 15 (war, Isaios VI.9).
[33] Cat. no.9, Isaios VII.14.
[34] The annulment of wills is treated in more detail in chapter 3 below.
[35] Cat. no.6, Isaios I.14.
[36] Cat. no.7, Isaios III.6, *pass.*
[37] Cat. no.15, Isaios VI.5,7
[38] At the age of 58 an Athenian citizen would be freed of his obligations to serve as a soldier. V.D.Hanson (1989, pp.89-95) has argued for a relatively large number of old men serving in the hoplite ranks. This, along with evidence that suggests that the Athenians would sometimes even call up men up to the age of 45 (Dem.III.4) makes me wary of suggesting a lower figure that would, in any case, be rather arbitrary, particularly since at least one of the testators concerned participated in warfare on his own initiative as a mercenary overseas (cat. no.11, Isaios IV.7). It is safe to infer, however, that the testators who set out on these expeditions were not about to breathe their last when they drew up their wills.
[39] **Sisters' sons or daughters:** cat. nos.7, 13, 15, 17; **sons of cousins:** Dikaiogenes III (cat. no.8) is normally held to have been the grandson of the adopter's, Dikaiogenes I's, paternal aunt (see Davies:1971,p.476). There is, however, no direct evidence for this blood-relationship apart from the fact that adopter and adoptee had the same name (see further the discussion in Cox:1988b). As for Xenainetos (cat.no. 10), he was in fact a natural brother of the testator, Aristarchos, but, *de jure*, son of

said with certainty not to have belonged to the ἀγχιστεῖαι of the testators[40]. It may be inferred from this that it was not unusual for a testator to choose a close relative as his beneficiary. Of course, that would not always prevent his will from being disputed by relatives who ranked even higher in the order of intestate succession than those who had been chosen for adoption: in all the attested cases of disputed wills, the wills were attacked by relatives of the deceased[41]. We have no examples of two wills which were tried against each other in an inheritance-case[42].

Half of the attested examples of testamentary adoption are known to us from speeches which were delivered in lawsuits having a direct bearing on the adoptions themselves[43]. Of the rest, at least two[44] are known to have been disputed at some point. In all these cases the persons opposing the wills were relatives who claimed to rank highest in the order of intestate succession. It is thus impossible to tell on the basis of the source-material available whether it was common practice to adopt an heir who would in any case have had the best claim to the inheritance of the testator by virtue of being his closest relative, even if a will had not been drawn up. A will in which such an intestate heir was chosen as beneficiary would presumably stand a better chance of being accepted without opposition than a will which disregarded the claims of the testator's closest relatives. If that is the case, there is a risk that the picture which emerges from the lawcourt speeches may be a distorted representation of how the Athenians adopted by will, since there is a

---

Aristarchos' cousin, since Aristarchos had been transferred to the οἶκος of his maternal grandfather's brother by means of adoption; **half-siblings**: cat. nos.9, 13.

[40] According to the speaker of Isaios IX, the adopted son of Astyphilos (cat. no.14) did not belong to Astyphilos' ἀγχιστεία, although he was the son of Astyphilos' cousin by blood. But the grandfather of the adoptee had been adopted into another οἶκος and had thus severed his ties to Astyphilos' family (Isaios IX.2). If the speaker of Isaios IV is to be believed, his opponent (cat. no.11) claimed to have been a fellow-soldier of his adoptive father, Nikostratos, an allegation which is opposed by the speaker (Isaios IV.26).

[41] Cat. nos.6, 8, 10, 11, 14, 15, 16.

[42] The closest we get to two wills being tried against each other is the case of Dikaiogenes II's will as described in Isaios V. According to the speaker, Dikaiogenes II's adopted son, Dikaiogenes III (cat. no.8), had originally claimed his inheritance on the basis of a will, according to which a third of the inheritance was bequeathed to the adoptee, while the sisters of Dikaiogenes II were to inherit the rest (Isaios V.6). Dikaiogenes III later produced a new will, in which he was made the universal heir of Dikaiogenes II, and had the first will overruled in favour of the second (Isaios V.15-16).

[43] Cat. nos.6, 8, 10, 11, 14, 15.

[44] Cat. nos.16 and 12.

much greater chance for a disputed will to have been mentioned in our sources than a will that went.unchallenged. The question of to what extent the Athenians used the will as a means of disrupting the order of intestate succession will be treated in more detail below in chapter 4. For now, it is only safe to conclude that the age of testators seemed to vary, some of them still having the prospect of begetting children, as for example Apollodoros, and that wills were often drawn up by men who faced imminent danger as soldiers or when travelling. As for their beneficiaries it is worth noting that the three female adoptees known to us were all adopted by will. And it would appear, too, that testators tended to choose their heirs from within their ἀγχιστεῖαι.

Posthumous adoption
The seven attested posthumous adoptions are more difficult to treat as a whole, since they seem to have been carried out under very different circumstances and do not show many common features. Several of them were claimed to have been illegal, but none of them was apparently ever disputed by a proper inheritance-suit in court while the adopted son was still alive[45]. It is extremely hard to tell which of the known posthumous adoptions were in fact legal, and who had the right to be adopted posthumously. It is also difficult to get an impression of who would be the "typical" adoptive father in a posthumous adoption.

Four of the seven adoptive fathers had been married[46], and three of them left daughters[47]. Only one of these daughters had been treated as an ἐπίκληρος ("heiress", see below, chapter 5), namely Euboulides' daughter Phylomache who was claimed by her cousin in an ἐπιδικασία[48]. In the other two cases the daughters had been married to men outside the family-circle before the posthumous adoptions had taken place. In both cases the adoptions were claimed to have been illegal, precisely because the adopted sons had allegedly violated the rights of the daughters involved, that is, the daughters had not been treated as

---

[45] Isaios X, in which the posthumous adoption of Aristarchos (cat. no.20) is attacked, was delivered only after the death of the adoptee. [Dem.] XLIV which is an attack on the posthumous adoption of Leochares (cat.no.18), was delivered in a δίκη ψευδομαρτυρίων ([Dem.] XLIV.45).
[46] Cat. nos.19, 20, 22, 24.
[47] Cat. nos. 19, 20, 24.
[48] [Dem.] XLIII.20, 55.

ἐπίκληροι⁴⁹. In one case it was a son born to the daughter who had been married off who attacked the adoption⁵⁰; in the other case it was the husbands of the daughters who tried to advance the claims on behalf of their wives⁵¹.

All the adopted sons, except one, belonged to the ἀγχιστεῖαι of their adoptive fathers. Diokles was, according to the speaker of Isaios VIII, the son born to his adoptive father's wife in a previous marriage⁵². Among the rest of the posthumously adopted persons we find one grandchild (daughter's son, cat. no.24), one nephew (sister's son, cat. no.23), and one who was legally the son of his adoptive father's niece (cat. no.20), but in fact the adoptee's natural grandchild (son's son). The last three cases are more difficult to penetrate. According to the speaker who delivered Isaios VI, an attempt was made to get two boys adopted posthumously into the οἶκοι of their paternal half-brothers⁵³. Moreover, their father was still alive at the time when the attempt was made⁵⁴. These two posthumous adoptions are in fact the only ones known to have been overruled by the People's Court, although not in an ἐπιδικασία⁵⁵. The third case is the one described in [Dem.] XLIV, that of Leochares who claimed to be the adopted son of his great-great-grandmother's brother, Archiades. This case differs from the rest in that the natural father of Leochares, Leostratos, had himself previously been the adopted son of Archiades, but he had exercised his right to return to the οἶκος of his own natural father, leaving a son to replace him in the οἶκος of the deceased⁵⁶. But the son died, and at his death Leostratos tried to regain his status as the adopted son of Archiades, according to the speaker of [Dem.] XLIV by attempting to force himself illegally onto the register of Archiades' deme⁵⁷. Leostratos failed in his

---

⁴⁹ Cat. nos.19 and 20.
⁵⁰ Isaios X.8, *pass.*
⁵¹ Isaios VIII.41.
⁵² Isaios VIII.40.
⁵³ Cat. nos.21 and 22.
⁵⁴ Isaios VI.35sq.
⁵⁵ According to the speaker of Isaios VI, Androkles approached the Archon on behalf of the two boys, claiming that these had been posthumously adopted, and that they were, accordingly, orphans (Isaios VI.36). Androkles and his conspirators claimed that they themselves were the boys' guardians, instigated a μίσθωσις οἴκου-procedure in the hope of being appointed lessees themselves at the auction (Isaios VI.36). Their plot was disclosed just as the auction was about to begin, and the judges refused to let out the property (καὶ οὕτως ἀπεχειροτόνησαν οἱ δικασταὶ μὴ μισθοῦν τοὺς οἴκους).
⁵⁶ [Dem.] XLIV.21sq.
⁵⁷ [Dem.] XLIV.35sqq.

attempt to get himself re-adopted even before the instigation of the lawsuit in which [Dem.] XLIV was delivered. Instead he tried to have his son Leochares adopted posthumously into Archiades' οἶκος[58], and this adoption was the one actually attacked in court by means of a δίκη ψευδομαρτυρίων.

As noted above, it is hard to get even a vague impression of the persons involved in the posthumous adoptions, because so many of these adoptions are claimed to have been illegal, but illegal in a different way from the adoptions carried out *inter vivos* or by will: unlike the attacks on adoptions of the latter two types, the attacks on posthumous adoptions could not be based on the provisions in the Solonic law on wills. The law was interpreted as conferring on the Athenians the right of choosing an heir employing either a will or adoption *inter vivos*, and only the mental state of the adopter, his position as a magistrate, or the fact that he had been acting under pressure or compulsion could render the act invalid, unless the adoptive father had natural sons at the time when he adopted. Most of these restrictions were not relevant to posthumous adoptions, because the adoptive father did not choose his heir himself; in fact, he was not involved in the procedure at all. Only the provision stating that an adopted son was not allowed to adopt, and that the right to adopt was restricted to those men who did not have natural sons would apply to the posthumous adoptions.

There may have been other rules which applied to this type of adoption, but we do not find them quoted or referred to by our sources. Even so, it may be safely assumed that the Athenians had some idea of which posthumous adoptions were legal and which were not, since the distinction is made quite clear in the forensic speeches. The question is on what criteria this distinction was made.

One may find the answer by looking at the two posthumous adoptions which were allegedly legal, namely the adoption of Makartatos into the οἶκος of his mother's brother and the adoption of Euboulides III into the οἶκος of his maternal grandfather[59]. The important common feature is that both adoptees were the intestate heirs of their adoptive fathers. Makartatos' mother had two brothers who both died without issue, and apparently she had no other siblings. She had had the inheritance awarded to her already before the adoption took place. Euboulides was

---

[58] [Dem.] XLIV.41sq.
[59] Cat. nos.23 and 24.

son of an ἐπίκληρος and had as such a claim on the inheritance left by his maternal grandfather.

Five of the posthumous adoptions were claimed to be illegal, and in three cases it is stated explicitly that the adopted son was *not* the intestate heir of the deceased[60] (in the last two cases the children are claimed to have been not only born out of wedlock, but the descendants of slaves. These two boys will be left out of the present discussion). In the case of Diokles, his adoptive father left daughters[61], and so did the adoptive father of Aristarchos II[62]. In both cases the adoptions were allegedly illegal because the rights of the daughters had been violated. Even an adoption performed *inter vivos* or on the basis of a will could be rendered invalid for this reason. As for the adoption of Leochares his opponents state repeatedly that his adoption was illegal: Leochares was not entitled to be adopted posthumously, because he, as well as his father, belonged to another οἶκος[63]. For this reason they were not allowed to carry out any posthumous adoption of an heir to Archiades' οἶκος, until after the inheritance had been the object of an ἐπιδικασία. If we compare this line of argument to the proposition advanced in the very same speech that a posthumous adoption should be carried out *after* the court's decision on who had the best claim[64], it would appear that posthumous adoption was conceived of as legal only if the adopted son had already been recognised by the People's Court as the heir with the best claim to the inheritance of his adoptive father[65].

The three examples of adopted sons who did not meet this requirement, not to speak of the two alleged bastards mentioned in Isaios VI, show that it was probably difficult to keep control over posthumous adoptions. In the following chapter it will be argued that it was the form of procedure itself which made abuse of this type of adoption possible.

---

[60] Cat. nos.18, 19, 20.
[61] Cat. no.19, see Isaios VIII.40 for reference to the daughters.
[62] Cat. no.20, see Isaios X.4sqq. for reference to the adopter's daughter.
[63] [Dem.] XLIV.33sq., 61.
[64] [Dem.] XLIV.43, 66.
[65] *Pace* Harrison (1968) who sees posthumous adoption as a possible antecedent to an ἐπιδικασία: "But if we take a test case and ask whether, if A dies intestate and childless and his estate is awarded to his next of kin B who has two sons, B could be forced by the archon to adopt one of the sons into A's house, the answer is probably no, *though if he did not he might find some other of the kin doing so and then claiming the estate on that basis.* (p.93, my italics). For a discussion of the rôle of the Archon in connection with posthumous adoptions, see chapter 6.

Adoption and social status

The conclusions drawn in the second section of this chapter have been very tentative, and there have been few attempts to make generalizations as to who would be the "typical" adopter or adoptee on the basis of the examples of adoptions compiled in the catalogue. One reason for being cautious is the relatively low number of adoptions known to us, as has already been stated above; another reason is that the evidence compiled in the catalogue throws light only on how wealthy Athenians practised adoption. In those cases where information is given concerning the size of the inheritance left by an adoptive father, the property does, as a rule, amount to more than one talent. Furthermore, four of the 25 attested adopters are known to have been liturgists. The smallest inheritance claimed to have been left by an adoptive father is that of Menekles: according to his adopted son, who delivered Isaios II, his property did not amount to more than 600 drachmas, an insignificant sum when compared to the other known estates which all ranged between 0.5 and four talents. The known adopters are listed along with the property which they left in table I below on page 30.

Table I: the properties of the known adoptive fathers.

Adopter	type of adoption	size of estate	APF no.	reference
Aischylos	?	?[66]	436=439	no information
Apollodoros	inter vivos	>3 talents	1395=1429	Isaios VII.6
Archephon	?	?	-	no information
Archiades	inter vivos ?	?[67]	5638C	no information
Archimachos	?	?	2921XIII	no information
Aristarchos I	posthumous	indebted?	-	Isaios X.16
Aristarchos II	testamentary	?	-	no information
Astyphilos	testamentary	?	7252C	no information
Dikaiogenes	testamentary	liturgist rent of property 80 m. a year	3773, p.146	Isaios V.11 Isaios V.36
Euboulides II	posthumous	?	2921VII	no information
Hagnias	testamentary	>2 talents	2921IX	Isaios XI.44
Hippolochides	?	?[68]	1395=1429, p.45	no information
Isokrates	inter vivos	liturgist	7716	Plut.*Vit X Orat.* 837C
Kleonymos	testamentary	?	-	no information
Lykophron	?	?	9251, pp.350sqq.	no information
Lysandros	?	?	6669, pp.217sqq.	no information
Makartatos I	posthumous	>3000 dr.	2921, pp.85sqq.	Isaios XI.49
Menekles	inter vivos	600 dr.	-	Isaios II.35
Nikostratos	testamentary	2 talents	7291, p.237	Isaios IV.7
Philoktemon	testamentary	liturgist[69]	15164, p.562	Isaios VI.27
Polyeuktos	inter vivos	? >100 mnas	-	Dem. XLI.3; 7-9; 27
Pyrrhos	testamentary	3 talents	-	Isaios III.2; 8; 18; 25; 80
Theophon	testamentary?	2,5 talents	2921, pp.84sqq.	Isaios XI.41;45
Xenainetos	?	>4 talents	-	Isaios X.23

The source material renders it impossible to decide whether poor Athenians or Athenians of modest means practised adoption in the same way as their rich fellow-citizens. The case of Menekles does not at all prove that poor Athenians, too, sometimes exercised their right to adopt. At the time when Menekles carried out his adoption, he was in possession of land worth 70 mnas[70], and his adopted son had served as a gymnasiarch after the adoption[71]. It is also worth remembering, for the sake of comparison, that only those Athenians whose property did not exceed 300 drachmas were eligible for the disablement pension.

---

[66] In IG II.2 417 the adopted son is recorded as having contributed 50 dr. as an *eutaxia* liturgist.
[67] Archiades' brother Archippos had been a trierarch ([Dem.] XLIV.9). Archippos died while his two brothers, Archiades and Meidylides, were still alive; thence his two brothers held the family estate jointly (ibid. 10). The speaker does not give any information concerning a later division of the property, nor does he refer to its size at the time of the trial in which he delivered his speech.
[68] Davies (1971), pp.46sq, identifies the adopted son with a Hippolochides Hippolochidou who served as a trierarch (IG II.2 1623, lines 237sq.).
[69] According to Isaios VI.38, Philoktemon and his father held the estate jointly.
[70] Isaios II.29.
[71] Isaios II.42.

Menekles left twice that amount, if we are to believe the speaker of Isaios II.

In chapter 4 it will be argued that the importance of adoption depended, at least to a certain extent, on the importance to the Athenian citizens of private tomb-cult. Now, it has been widely assumed that private tomb-cult was associated with wealth. However, this position has been questioned more recently, especially by S.C. Humphreys in her article "Family Tombs and Tomb Cult in Ancient Athens". Here she argues that in the IV. century it was not a privilege of the rich; during the V. and IV. centuries, the whole institution had undergone a democratization[72].

Another reason for adopting an heir was to ensure γηροτροφία, to be provided for in one's old age. It is unlikely that ordinary citizens would be less dependent on support from their descendants than the rich, who would often be able to live on the interests of their estates.

Thus, there is no immediate reason to assume that ordinary Athenians would be less motivated to adopt than the wealthy part of the population which is represented in the forensic speeches. But even if this is true (and it cannot be proved), it may be argued that the incentive for letting oneself be adopted into a poor man's οἶκος was probably small, especially when considering that the adoptee would have to relinquish the inheritance left by his natural father. On the other hand, if the adopter left but a modest inheritance, his adoption would probably stand a much better chance of being accepted without resistance from other heirs, assuming that the eagerness to contest an adoption on the part of the intestate heirs would grow with the size of the property at stake. The case decribed in Isaios II may of course be used to refute this assumption, for, according to the speaker, the fact that Menekles left only 600 drachmas did not prevent his brother from attacking the adoption.

Now, it is more than likely that Menekles' property was in fact considerably larger than stated by the speaker[73] (who found it

---

[72] Reprinted in Humphreys (1983b), pp.79-130, see also Th.Heine Nielsen et al.(1989).

[73] Even so, the person who delivered the διαμαρτυρία on behalf of Menekles' adopted son would have had to pay a deposit amounting to 10% of the inheritance. This may mean that we can have greater confidence in the figure given in Isaios II. On the παρακαταβολή being obligatory in connection with the διαμαρτυρία, see e.g. the discussions in Gernet (1955), pp.87-89 and Harrison (1971), p.181-183. The only evidence for the percentage due in private law-suits is Pollux VIII.39 (quoted by Harrison (1971), p.180, n.4).

worthwhile to pay Isaios to write his speech!); moreover, the speaker emphasises that his opponent is behaving in an unusual and mean way by attacking his adoption without having anything to gain from it financially.

These speculations, however, can only lead to the rather disappointing conclusion that we can neither rule out nor confirm that adoption was practised by Athenians belonging to all social strata of Athenian society. This is important to bear in mind when using the data compiled in the catalogue. They only tell us of how the most wealthy Athenians used adoption as a remedy against their childlessness.

Chapter 3: Procedures of adoption

In this chapter the different procedures of the three types of adoption will be dealt with. It will soon become apparent that the procedures have many common features, and for this reason they will all be treated together rather than in three different sub-sections.

A convenient starting-point for the discussion will be the brief description of how an adoption *inter vivos* was carried out which is to be found in Isaios II.12 sqq. The childless Menekles had asked the brothers of his ex-wife if one of them would consent to being adopted by him, and it was agreed that the speaker who delivered Isaios II was to be Menekles' adopted son "and in this way he adopted me" (καὶ ἐκ τοῦ τρόπου τούτου ποιεῖταί με, 12). Thence, the speaker recounts, "he adopted me, not by writing it in a will... but, being in good health and of perfectly sound mind, he adopted me and introduced me to his phratry in the presence of my opponents, and got me enrolled as a member of his deme and of his *orgeon*-group[1]." (...ἐμὲ ποιεῖται, οὐκ ἐν διαθήκαις, ὦ ἄνδρες, γράψας... ἀλλ' ὑγιαίνων, εὖ φρονῶν, εὖ νοῶν ποιησάμενος εἰσάγει με εἰς τοὺς φράτερας παρόντων τούτων, καὶ εἰς τοὺς δημότας με ἐγγράφει καὶ εἰς τοὺς ὀργεῶνας. 14)[2].

On the basis of this description, many modern scholars have seen the procedure of adoption as consisting of two main phases: a private phase, which in Menekles' case consisted of his agreement with his ex-brother-

---

[1] For the discussion of the connection between phratries and orgeones, see e.g. A. Andrewes (1961) and F. Bourriot (1976), Vol.I, pp.595-663, esp.654-657.
[2] The translation of the chiasmus ποιεῖται : γράψας : : ποιησάμενος : εἰσάγει has caused me some problems. The argument that the private agreement was the act that juridically constituted an Athenian adoption rests partly on interpreting the aorist participle ποιησάμενος as describing an action which took place prior to the action described by the finite verb in the historical present tense, εἰσάγει. This is the most straightforward reading of the second part of the chiasmus; but if one insists on this temporal sequence, the first part of the chiasmus becomes hard to understand. For in that case it ought to be translated "He adopted me, not *after having written* it in a will", which does not make sense, since the speaker represents the writing of a will as the very last act of a dying man. Indeed, the first clause call for the translation "He adopted me, not *by writing* a will", and the whole passage may be translated with reference to the observation made by Goodwin in *Syntax of the Moods and Tenses of the Greek Verb*, §150, p.52: "An aorist participle denoting that in which the action of a verb of past tense consists may express time coincident with that of the verb, when the actions of the verb and the participle are practically one." (See further section 2 of this chapter, below).

in-law, and a public phase, consisting in the adopted son being enrolled as a member of the adopter's phratry and deme. In the following paragraphs these two phases will be dealt with separately, and it will be argued that it was the public phase, that is, the enrolment of the adoptee in the phratry and deme of his adoptive father, which constituted the actual procedure of adoption.

1. The private agreement

A parallel to the private agreement described in Isaios II.12 is found in Isaios VII.14. This speech was delivered in defence of Apollodoros' adoption of his half-sister's son, Thrasyllos. According to Thrasyllos who delivered the speech, Apollodoros entrusted the administration of his property to him immediately after the conclusion of their private agreement[3]. Some modern scholars have argued on the basis of these two Isaios-passages that it was the private agreement between adopter and adoptee (or the latter's κύριος, if he was a minor) that was the essential part of an adoption, and they claim that the private agreement itself was enough legally to validate the adoption[4]. The private agreement would have formed part only of an adoption *inter vivos*, whereas the drawing up of a will was a unilateral legal act. Since not even witnesses were required for a will to be valid, it would have been technically possible that the person who had been named as adoptee in a will was wholly ignorant of the arrangements made by the testator, until the will was produced after the testator's death. (But it has been noted that while there is evidence that some testators did not call witnesses to the contents of their wills[5], there is no evidence for testators who omitted to call witnesses who could later testify to the *existence* of their wills). It has been claimed that it was precisely the unilateral nature of the will which necessitated that it be confirmed by the People's Court

---

[3] Isaios VII.15.
[4] See e.g. Beauchet (1897), vol.II, pp.10sq., 18sq. ; Bruck (1909) pp.54sqq. with the reservation that "Perfekt wurde der Akt in beiden fällen erst mit der Eintragung des Adoptierten in die "Civilstandsregister", in die Phratorenliste und das Bürgerbuch" (p.54 n.3); Lipsius (1905-15), vol.I, p.514 followed by Becker (1932), p.301 and 306; Brindesi (1961), pp.45sq.; Poláček (1967), p.162, Harrison (1968), p.89.
[5] This is what is claimed in Isaios IV.13 and [Dem.] XLVI.28. We may infer from these passages that it would seem at least plausible to the judges that a testator might wish to keep secret the contents of his will.

before the beneficiary could be recognised as the adopted son of the deceased[6]. According to this view, an adoption carried out *inter vivos* was regarded as a contract between two parties, adopter and adoptee, and a contract, oral as well as written, was considered legally valid in Athens if both parties had made a mutual declaration of intent[7]. Therefore an adoption *inter vivos, qua* contract, was a complete and valid legal act, which the will was not. It will be argued below that testamentary adoption *was* probably considered incomplete at the death of the testator, and that this caused some procedural disadvantages for the person adopted in a will, but it will also be argued that it was not the unilateral nature of the will which was the reason for this. Rather, the answer must be sought in the public sphere, the demes and the phratries, whose acceptance of the adoptee may have been crucial for his legal rights.

As to posthumous adoption, it does not seem to have been requisite that the deceased had stated, orally or in writing, his wish that a person succeed him as his adopted son after his death. It appears from Isaios III.73 that a man could state his wish that a posthumous adoption would later take place; but the posthumous adoption of Makartatos II was alleged to have been carried out at the request of the sister of the deceased, and it is not claimed that the "adopter", Makartatos I, had expressed any wish to this effect before his death[8]. Thus, posthumous adoption could be carried out without the adoptive father's having played any part in the procedure at all.

---

[6] For references, see n.4. See also Gernet (1955), p.123.

[7] Dem. LVI.2: τῷ οὖν ποτὲ πιστεύοντες καὶ τί λαβόντες τὸ βέβαιον, προϊέμεθα; ὑμῖν, ὦ ἄνδρες δικασταί, καὶ τοῖς νόμοις τοῖς ὑμετέροις, οἳ κελεύουσιν, ὅσα ἂν τις ἑκὼν ἕτερος ἑτέρῳ ὁμολογήσῃ, κύρια εἶναι. Wolff (1957) has argued convincingly against the traditional interpretation of this passage and concludes (p.61): "Mit dem Konsensualvertrag im Sinne eines Zusammenklangs mehrerer auf Herstellung obligatorischer Bindungen gerichteter Willenserklärungen hatte die griechische Homologie nichts zu tun".

[8] In Isaios XI.49, Theopompos claims that it was his wife who had persuaded him to carry out the posthumous adoption of Makartatos II (cat. no.23). This passage will be treated in more detail in chapter 6, section 2.

2. Enrolment in phratry and deme

In Isaios VII.15sqq. the procedure which an adopted son had to go through at his enrolment in the phratry of his adoptive father is described in detail. The procedure of admission to the phratry in question was the same whether the son to be enrolled was a natural son or an adopted son. The (adoptive) father swore with his hand on the sacrificial animal that the (adopted) son was born from a married citizen-woman. Thereupon the phrateres would vote on the admission of the candidate, and only after they had cast their votes could the candidate be entered on the phratry register.

The speaker begins his description of this procedure with the remark: "With them (i.e. Apollodoros' phrateres) the same law applies both when someone introduces a natural son, and when he introduces an adopted son..." (ἔστι δ' αὐτοῖς νόμος ὁ αὐτός, ἐάν τέ τινα φύσει γεγονότα εἰσάγῃ τις, ἐάν τε ποιητόν...) This may be interpreted to the effect that the rules of admission could vary from phratry to phratry, and that some phratries may have had special rules pertaining to the admission of adopted sons as opposed to natural sons.

However, the other sources which inform us of procedures of admission into Athenian phratries, be it of natural or adopted sons, seem to agree with the description given in Isaios VII. Unfortunately, the most detailed of these, the decrees of the Demotionidai (IG II 1237) deal only very superficially with the actual admission (εἰσαγωγή) of the candidates, while the scrutiny (διαδικασία) following the admission is treated in detail in the inscription[9]. The important thing to note here is that the document, in spite of its detailed drafting, does not mention any special rules regulating the admission of adopted sons. Although the evidence for the phratries' procedures of admission is much too scarce to allow the conclusion that the procedure of admission was the same in any given phratry, it is safe to assume that the procedure described in Isaios VII was neither unique nor uncommon.

A phratry-member who wished to oppose the adoption could object to it during the procedure and thus influence the outcome of the phrateres' voting on the candidate. In [Dem.] XLIII.14 it is claimed that it was possible for an opponent to bar the admission altogether by removing the sacrificial animal from the altar.

---

[9] I follow the interpretation suggested by Hedrick (1990).

If the phratry refused to admit the candidate, this decision could probably be appealed to the People's Court. The right of appeal to the People's Court of an adverse vote is not stated in the decrees of the Demotionidai, which only mention the possibility of appeal *within* the phratry[10]. But in [Dem.] LIX.60 there is evidence that a phratry's decision could be appealed to the People's Court, if the phratry had refused to admit a natural son. A passage in [Dem.] XLIII.82 allows the assumption that the decision of the phratry could also be appealed if the candidate was an adopted son: "And when he was introduced, the other phratry-members cast their votes in secret, but Makartatos here cast his vote, clear for all to see, that this boy was to be introduced lawfully as a son for Euboulides in that he did not wish to make himself responsible (ὑπεύθυνος) by touching the sacrificial animal or leading it away from the altar; no! he took his share of the meat from this boy and went away just like all the other phrateres." (καὶ ὅτε εἰσήγετο, οἱ μὲν ἄλλοι φράτερες κρύβδην ἔφερον τὴν ψῆφον, οὑτοσὶ δὲ Μακάρτατος φανερᾷ τῇ ψήφῳ ἐψηφίσατο ὀρθῶς εἰσάγεσθαι Εὐβουλίδῃ υἱόν τὸν παῖδα τουτονί, οὐκ ἐθελήσας ἅψασθαι τοῦ ἱερείου οὐδὲ ἀπαγαγεῖν ἀπὸ τοῦ βωμοῦ ὑπεύθυνον αὐτὸν ποιήσας, ἀλλὰ καὶ τὴν μερίδα τῶν κρεῶν ᾤχετο λαβὼν παρὰ τοῦ παιδὸς τουτουί, ὥσπερ καὶ οἱ ἄλλοι φράτερες.) Makartatos could have been held responsible, if he had prevented the admission of Euboulides' adopted son into the phratry. It cannot be determined, however, whether Makartatos could be drawn to account by means of an appeal to the People's Court, or whether appeal was possible within the phratry only. But this passage is important in that it shows that the decision to turn down a candidate for adoption could indeed be appealed. And since we know that the decision to turn down a candidate introduced *qua* natural son could be appealed to the People's Court as well as within the phratry, it is likely that the same would apply to an adopted son. But there are no examples of adopted sons or their adoptive fathers actually exercising this right, so the question cannot be answered with certainty.

As to the admission of adopted sons into the deme of their adoptive fathers, the sources yield but little information. In Isaios VII.28 we are told that the deme-members were to swear an oath before the vote on admission of the candidate could take place, and that the admission of the adopted son, at this event, took place at the deme-assembly where

---

[10] ll.94-100 concerning the "regular scrutiny" according to Hedrick's interpretation (1990), pp.71sqq.

the deme-magistrates were elected. In [Dem.] XLIV.35sqq. an account is given of how Leostratos attempted to get himself enrolled as Archiades' adopted son in the latter's deme and failed. This also took place at the deme-assembly where election of magistrates was on the agenda, and Whitehead has pointed out that the demes could reduce the number of regular deme-assemblies to one a year by dealing with admissions and elections at the same session.[11] We are told that the demotai of Archiades' deme also swore an oath before they cast their vote, and both accounts referred to here are in accordance with what we are told in *Ath.Pol.* 42.1 about the admission of new deme-members in general. There is thus no reason to assume that the admission of an adopted son into the deme of the adopter would differ essentially from that of a natural son[12], although Whitehead may be right in assuming that a grown-up adopted son would not have to undergo δοκιμασία by the βουλή, since it had already previously been certified that he had reached the age of 18[13]. It is further stated in *Ath.Pol.* 42.1 that a rejected candidate could appeal the decision of the deme to the People's Court. An adopted son may have been on a par with a natural son in this respect (see above), but, again, we know of no concrete instance where an adopted son exercised this right of appeal, so we must leave the question open.

Presumably, it was only when adopting *inter vivos* that the adopter would get the adoptee enrolled in his phratry and deme while he himself was still alive. Even so, a person adopted by will would have to be enrolled as the son of his adoptive father in the latter's phratry and deme as well[14]. It is remarkable, however, that there are no references to these procedures in the forensic speeches which were delivered in

---

[11] (1986), p.92.

[12] In Menander's *Samia*, v.10, Demeas' adopted son states that he has been inscribed (in Demeas' deme?) οὐδὲν διαφέρων οὐδενὸς. However, the meaning of this passage has been disputed, and the readings ἐτράφην and οὐκ ἐξετράφην have been suggested instead of]ἐγράφην. See Gomme and Sandbach (1973), pp.545sq. But palaeographically there is little doubt that the second letter after the lacuna is a γ and not a τ. I am grateful to Dr. A.Bülow-Jacobsen for having stated his opinion as a papyrologist on the basis of a photograph of the passage in question.

[13] (1986), p.103 with n.89.

[14] Isaios X.9. The speaker claims that an adoptee was allowed to be enrolled in the adopter's deme only if he was adopted by will. So the passage may be interpreted to the effect that the speaker does in fact deny that posthumous adoption was possible. The speaker tries to prove that the adoptee could not have been adopted by will and that there was thus no legal basis for his having been enrolled in the adopter's phratry. The speaker's allegation may be countered by a reference to cat. nos.23 and 24.

disputes over testamentary adoptions[15], not least if we compare these speeches to those delivered as either attacks on or in defence of adoptions carried out *inter vivos* or posthumously[16]. In the latter, phratry-enrolment in particular is given a rather prominent place in the argumentation. It is therefore possible to argue *e silentio* that these procedures of enrolment had not yet been carried out at the time when the sons adopted by will had to defend, in the People's Court, the validity of the wills providing for their adoptions.

It is, in fact, generally agreed that a person adopted by will had to have the will ratified formally by an inheritance-procedure (ἐπιδικασία), before he could be enrolled in his adoptive father's phratry and deme. From the description given in *Ath. Pol.* 43.4 and from a narrative passage in [Dem.] XLIII.5 we get an impression of how the procedure was initiated: from *Ath. Pol.* it appears that the claims (λήξεις) made on inheritances were to be read out in the assembly "so that no-one should be ignorant of any inheritance being vacant." (ὅπως μηδένα λάθη μηδὲν ἔρημον γενόμενον). This was a fixed point on the agenda of the ἐκκλησία κυρία. We must assume that the claimant(s) initiated this procedure by approaching the Archon stating his (their) claim in writing, and that further steps in the ἐπιδικασία-procedure were only made when the claim had been announced in public[17]. If more claimants appeared, the

---

[15] Isaios I, IV, VI, IX, X (the references made in X to phratry-enrolment have a bearing on the allegedly illegal posthumous adoption of the testator himself.) Isaios III and V are also dealing with testamentary adoptions, but they differ from the rest in that the adoptees had already been acknowledged as adoptees for many years prior to the delivery of the speeches. Isaios V.47 suggests that Dikaiogenes had got a new identity as a citizen as a result of his adoption; for one thing he had to renounce the privileges accruing to the descendants of the tyrant-slayers. Cf. [Dem.] LVIII.30sq. (the case of Charidemos will be treated in section 4 of this chapter), and see Wyse (1904), p.482.
[16] Isaios II and VII, [Dem.] XLIII and XLIV.
[17] I follow Hansen, (1983) p.15 with n.53 *pace* E.Karabelias (1974), p. 209 n.29 and Harrison (1968), p.159 n.4. Harrison argues that the announcement referred to by the speaker in [Dem.] XLIII.5 was made *after* the court had adjudicated the inheritance to a claimant, since in the particular instance, which the speaker recounts, the claimants had to make a deposit, a παρακαταβολή. Therefore it must be a reopening of the case, which the speaker is talking about. And he infers "that the announcement by the herald was made at the moment when the court had made its adjudication". This seems rather bad economy on the part of the Athenians. It would be more logical if the announcement was made prior to the adjudication in order to make sure that all potential claimants would come forward so as to avoid endless reopenings of the inheritance-suit. In fact, the speaker telescopes his account of the lawsuits prior to his present case; what he does *not* tell is that already when Phylomache, Glaukon, and other claimants disputed over Hagnias' inheritance, it had previously been awarded to Hagnias' niece who had died childless (Isaios XI.8-11). So even at this point all claimants had to make a deposit, since the inheritance-suit was formally considered to be reopened. Cf. Thompson (1976), pp.16sq.

People's Court would decide on who had the best claim. It is disputed what would happen if only one claimant turned up. Some scholars have argued that the Archon would adjudicate the inheritance to him as a purely administrative decision[18], while others have maintained that the People's Court would in any case have to adjudicate the inheritance formally to the claimant[19]. Although there is no decisive evidence with which this scholarly dispute may be settled, it must be pointed out that formal confirmations formed an important part of the functions of the People's Court, in addition to the settling of disputes[20]. It is therefore unsafe to assume *a priori* that the People's Court would only have been involved if the vacant inheritance became an object of dispute between two or more parties.

A natural son who had been born in wedlock could take possession of his father's property (ἐμβατεύειν) without having had his right to it confirmed by an ἐπιδικασία[21]. Moreover, it was possible for him to bar any inheritance-procedure instigated by another claimant by employing the procedure of διαμαρτυρία: he himself[22] or another person on his behalf[23] could state formally that the inheritance could not be made the object of an ἐπιδικασία, since the deceased had left a son born in wedlock, a γνήσιος υἱός. Thence other claimants would have to bring a law-suit against the witness for bearing false testimony, a δίκη ψευδομαρτυρίων, if they wanted to uphold their claim to the inheritance. It is not known whether the interrupted ἐπιδικασία would be reopened if the prosecutors won the δίκη ψευδομαρτυρίων. It is possible that the inheritance would be awarded to the successful prosecutors straight away if they could prove that the defendant was not a γνήσιος υἱός after all[24].

A son who had been adopted *inter vivos* was, in this respect, on a par with a natural son: he also had the right to ἐμβάτευσις[25]. But the inheritance of a man who left neither natural sons nor a son adopted *inter vivos* had always to be the object of an ἐπιδικασία, no matter whether he had left a will or not[26]. Thus a son adopted by will was in

---

[18] E.g. H.J. Wolff (1946), pp.70sq., MacDowell (1978), pp.102sq.
[19] Lipsius (1905-15), p.581, Gernet (1955) p.69, n.3, 71, Harrison (1968), pp.159sq. with ref. to previous discussion on p.159, n.5.
[20] See e.g. Hansen (1991), pp.179sq.
[21] E.g. Isaios VIII.34.
[22] [Dem.] XLIV.29, 42sq., 53 sqq.
[23] Isaios II.2, 17; V.16.
[24] For references to the discussion, see Harrison (1968), pp.156sq.
[25] [Dem.] XLIV.19.
[26] Isaios III.60, VI.3, [Dem.] XLIII.5, XLVI.23, Dio.Hal. *De Isaeo*, 15.

this respect on a par with the collaterals of the deceased; he was not considered a descendant. It will be argued below that the reason why the position of a son adopted by will differed from that of a son adopted *inter vivos* was that the former was not considered an adopted son with the rights of a descendant, before he had been enrolled successfully in the phratry and deme of the testator. And this could only happen when he had had the inheritance awarded to him by the People's Court.

Posthumous adoption differed procedurally from the two other types first and foremost in that the adoptive father need not have stated his wish to adopt at all for the adoption to be carried out. MacDowell stated in his *The Law in Classical Athens* [27] that the "details of the procedure of posthumous adoption are obscure", and, as noted earlier, it is, indeed, very hard to determine exactly how a posthumous adoption was carried out, because so many of the known examples were allegedly illegal. Some scholars assume that a posthumous adoption had to be ratified by the Archon or the People's Court, before the adopted son was allowed to succeed to the inheritance of his adoptive father[28], but a closer analysis of the available evidence, especially the posthumous adoption described in [Dem.] XLIII, will show that this was probably not the case.

[Dem.] XLIII was delivered in one of the law-suits concerning the inheritance left by Hagnias. Hagnias had died childless, and his property was to be the object of numerous inheritance-suits. The dispute over his inheritance went on for many years[29], but the ἐπιδικασία in which [Dem.] XLIII was delivered is the latest law-suit known to us. We cannot tell with certainty what was the outcome of this last ἐπιδικασία, although

---

[27] p.101.
[28] E.g. Ruschenbusch (1962), p.309, n.7; Harrison (1968), p.95. Becker (1932) has made the observation that the persons eligible for posthumous adoption were those who had the best claim to the inheritance according to the law on intestate succession. In his sketchy account on p.302 he assumes that the candidate for a posthumous adoption would already have been selected (by a family-council?) before having the inheritance awarded to him: "In beiden Fällen wird der Berufene *wie ein Erbe* durch epidikasie in den Nachlaß eingewiesen und posthum *durch die Anchisten* vor Phratrie und Demos adoptiert" (my italics). Becker seems to assume that the candidate for adoption was chosen by the ἀγχιστεῖς, but he does not reconstruct the Athenian procedure of posthumous adoption in any detail, and it is hard to guess what was his actual hypothesis in this respect.
[29] [Dem.] XLIII is dated to c.345 by Thompson (1976), p.63 on the basis of the ephebic roster referred to in n.30, below. Thompson (1976: p.12) dates Hagnias' death to 396 identifying Hagnias with the ambassador Hagnias who is mentioned in the *Hellenica Oxyrhynchia* 7.1. This identification has been doubted by Humpreys (1983a) who prefers a date in the 370's (375 or 373) for Hagnias' death.

there are indications[30] that the speaker lost his case, or rather the case he had instigated on behalf of his natural son, Euboulides III. This Euboulides, still a minor[31], had been adopted into the οἶκος of his maternal grandfather, Euboulides II. And what is important to us in this respect is that the adoption itself formed the basis of Euboulides III's claim on Hagnias' inheritance. Euboulides II is claimed to have been Hagnias' first cousin, and was as such a member of Hagnias' ἀγχιστεία. The Athenian ἀγχιστεία included relatives as far removed as children of first cousins[32]. Euboulides II's grandchild Euboulides III was not a member of Hagnias' ἀγχιστεία, but by being adopted as his grandfather's son he moved up one generation and could then advance his claim *qua* son of Hagnias' cousin. This adoption is therefore of immense importance to the speaker's argumentation, and we must assume that the speaker did his best to show that the adoption of Euboulides was legal, and that it had been carried out correctly. And the speaker does in fact relate in great detail how Euboulides III was enrolled in his grandfather's phratry[33]. On the other hand, he does not mention at all that the adoption had been ratified by any *other* procedure. In the light of the context outlined above, we can safely assume *e silentio* that the procedure of posthumous adoption, in the case of Euboulides III, had consisted solely in his admission into the phratry of Euboulides II. If the adoption had been ratified by more procedures, e.g. by the Archon or by the People's Court, the speaker would only have helped his cause by including them all in his account.

Likewise, in Isaios X, where the speaker attempts to prove that the posthumous adoption of Aristarchos had been illegal, he uses on three

---

[30] Ἁγνίας Μακαρτάτου ἐξ Οἴου is listed in an ephebic roster of 324/3 (*Arch.Eph.* 1918, pp.73-100 = Reinmuth, *The Ephebic Inscriptions of the Fourth Century B.C.*, Leiden 1971, no.15). The name might well indicate that the descendants of Theopompos were still in control of Hagnias' inheritance (thus Broadbent (1968), p.62 and Thompson (1976), p.107).

[31] [Dem.] XLIII.15.

[32] The wording μέχρι ἀνεψιῶν παίδων in the law of intestate succession (quoted in [Dem.] XLIII.51) can be interpreted in two different ways, meaning both the sons of the cousin of the *de cujus*, that is, *first cousins once removed*, and *second cousins*. The meaning was apparently ambiguous already in the IV. century (so Schaps (1975), p.54 n.3, which is the solution I prefer). In [Dem.] XLIII, Sositheos' interpretation is clearly that of first cousin once removed. But Theopompos had the estate of Hagnias awarded to him, although he was not the son of Hagnias' cousin; however, he and Hagnias were *sons of cousins* (Isaios XI.8). Thompson argued that Theopompos' interpretation was the correct one (1976, pp.4-8 and 20-22) *pace* Wyse (1904), p.674 and Davies (1971), p.79. See further E.Karabelias (1982), p.58 for references to the modern debate on which interpretation is to be preferred.

[33] [Dem.] XLIII.11-15 and 81sq.

occasions the wording εἰς τοὺς φράτερας εἰσαχθῆναι to denote the adoption as such[34]. This indicates that the enrolment in the phratry of the adoptive father could sometimes be construed as the actual procedure of adoption.

The fact that six out of eight known cases of posthumous adoption were alleged to have been illegal strongly indicates that this type of adoption was hard to control. This also points to the conclusion that ratification by means of ἐπιδικασία was not obligatory.

Moreover, it must be noted that we do not know of any case where a posthumous adoption had been attacked by means of ἐπιδικασία while the adopted son was still alive. There is one example of claimants opposing a posthumous adoption who *tried* to instigate an ordinary inheritance-suit, but when the adopted son met their claim with a διαμαρτυρία, they had to resort to a δίκη ψευδομαρτυρίων instead[35]. The single known example of ἐπιδικασία having been employed in order to challenge a posthumous adoption was only instigated when the adopted son had died childless leaving a will[36]. In these two cases the argument of the parties opposing the adoptions is based largely on the claim that the adopted sons had not been entitled to be posthumously adopted[37]. Had it been *obligatory* for posthumously adopted sons to have their adoptions ratified by ἐπιδικασία one would expect that at least some of the posthumous adoptions known to us would at some point have been attacked by means of this procedure in the lifetime of the adopted sons.

It may seem strange that a posthumously adopted son had the right to succeed to the property of his adoptive father without having had his adoption ratified by the People's Court in advance, considering that this was denied to the son who had been adopted by will. Compare, for example, the reasoning of Harrison: "Those adopted by will, on the other hand, could not enter, but had to state their claim before the archon,...*A fortiori* those adopted posthumously could not enter without reference to the archon."[38] But the explanation is probably to be found

---

[34] Isaios X.8, 15, 21.
[35] [Dem.] XLIV.34 and 45.
[36] Isaios X.2.
[37] [Dem.] XLIV.26, 38, 40, 43, Isaios X.8, 9, 11, 12, 14, 15.
[38] (1968), p.95. Ruschenbusch (1962) argues as follows (p.309 n.7): "Dabei ist beachtenswert daß die adoptio postume *rechtlich bedeutungslos* ist. Während der *inter vivos* Adoptierte die Erbschaft wie ein leiblicher Sohn einfach auf dem Wege der Embateusis antritt, ist beim postum Adoptierten der Antritt der Erbschaft *vom Zuspruch des Archon abhängig*" (my italics).

in what was pointed out in the previous chapter, namely that the adopted sons in the putatively legal cases of posthumous adoptions were the *intestate heirs* of their adoptive fathers, and that they had been recognised as such by means of ἐπιδικασία before the adoptions were carried out. As the son of an ἐπίκληρος who had been the object of an ἐπιδικασία, Euboulides was by law entitled to his grandfather's inheritance without recourse to the People's Court before entering upon it[39]. And Makartatos II's mother had had her brother's, Makartatos I's, inheritance awarded to her by an ἐπιδικασία; as her legitimate male descendant, Makartatos II was entitled to take over the property of his uncle without recourse to the People's Court[40]. This solution is corroborated by the repeated statement of the speaker in [Dem.] XLIV: the οἶκος of Archiades ought to be continued by means of posthumous adoption, when the court had decided who was to be considered heir to his inheritance, *and only then* [41].

On this basis it will be concluded that 1) the right to be adopted posthumously was restricted to those intestate heirs who had already had the inheritance awarded to them by ἐπιδικασία, and that 2) the procedure of posthumous adoption consisted solely in that a person, who had had the inheritance awarded to him by ἐπιδικασία, was subsequently enrolled as son of the deceased in the latter's phratry (and deme, if the adoptee was an adult[42]). The most important difference between the procedure of posthumous adoption and that of adoption *inter vivos* was that the adoptive father in the first case had not himself chosen his adopted son. An important common feature is that the People's Court was not necessarily involved in the procedure of adoption. The phratry's and deme's acceptance of the adopted son was apparently sufficient to render the adoption legally valid.

As for the alleged abuse of this procedure, corruption in phratries and demes may explain why it happened that persons were adopted although they were not entitled to be.[43]

---

[39] [Dem.] XLIII.13; for the rights of the sons of ἐπίκληροι, see ch. 5.
[40] Isaios XI.49
[41] [Dem.] XLIV.36, 40, 43, 66.
[42] [Dem.] XLIV.35-41
[43] Tampering with the procedure of enrolment into these two bodies (or striking citizens off the registers) is a commonplace, e.g. Aisch. I.114, Isaios VI.22-25, [Dem.]XLIV.37-42, Dem. LVII.8-14 For corruption in demes, see also *Ath.Pol.*62.1 on demes selling magistracies. See further Whitehead (1986), pp.291-301 and his collection of evidence from comedy, pp.327-345. He points out a possible difference between small and large demes in regard to the level of corruption.

In the light of this argument it is not reasonable to treat the enrolment of an adopted son in the phratry and deme of the adopter as a mere confirmation of the adoption in the presence of as many witnesses as possible[44]. The existence of posthumous adoption in the form presented above suggests that the role played by the phratries and demes in the procedure of adoption is to be upgraded. In the next section of this chapter it will be argued that they are to be given a central place therein.

3. Effects of the three procedures of adoption

The most important effect of an adoption was to make the adopted son the heir of his adoptive father. Another consequence was that he lost his right to succeed to the inheritance left by his natural father[45]. He also lost the right to inherit from his natural father's relatives[46]. But according to the speaker who delivered Isaios VII, he did not lose his connection with his mother, and it would still be possible for him to succeed to property left by his mother's relatives[47].

In the previous section it has been stated that the legal position of a son who had been adopted *inter vivos* differed considerably from that of a person who had been adopted by will. The former had the right to immediate succession to the inheritance left by his adoptive father, ἐμβάτευσις. He could prevent other claimants from instigating an ἐπιδικασία by means of the procedure of διαμαρτυρία, stating formally that the deceased had left a γνήσιος υἱός. He was thus procedurally on the same footing as a natural son who had been born in wedlock. But a testamentary adoption did not give the adopted son the right to ἐμβάτευσις. If the adopted son took possession of the inheritance left by the testator before the will had been ratified by ἐπιδικασία, he committed

---

[44] See e.g. Beauchet (1897), vol.II, p.11 and pp.18sq., Polácek (1967), p.162, and Harrison (1968) p.89.
[45] E.g. Isaios IX.33 and X.4 (see also Dem.LVIII.30-32 which is discussed in section 4 of this chapter). A man who had incurred ἀτιμία as a state-debtor could prevent his sons' inheriting his debt and ἀτιμία by having them adopted into other οἶκοι (Isaios X.17, and ch.2 above).
[46] Isaios VII.23, IX.2.
[47] Isaios VII.25.

an offence[48]. He was, in other words, procedurally of the same standing as the collaterals of the deceased. It has been suggested above that it was the enrolment of the son adopted *inter vivos* in the phratry and deme of the adopter *in the adopter's lifetime* which was the reason why a son thus adopted enjoyed the rights of a descendant. The aim of this section is to attempt to corroborate this statement, after the traditional explanation of this problem has been considered.

Scholars have attached much importance to the contractual relationship entered into by the adopter and the adoptee (or the latter's κύριος) in connection with an adoption *inter vivos*, that is, to the private agreement which has been treated in the first section of this chapter. Since an adoption *inter vivos* was considered a contract, it was as such a complete and valid legal act which did not require ratification by the Archon or the People's Court. A testator, on the other hand, could adopt an heir without the heir's consent.[49] Thus, a testamentary adoption could not be considered a contract, and for this reason the making of a will was an incomplete legal act which would have to be confirmed by the People's Court before taking effect. In his "La loi de Solon sur le 'testament'" Gernet argues that the testamentary adoption was a secondarily developed variant of the original Solonian adoption: adoption *inter vivos*. The fact that a son adopted by will did not have the right of ἐμβάτευσις indicates, according to Gernet, that the Athenians as late as in the IV. century did not consider an adoption by will a *proper*, that is a contractual, adoption.[50] My reason for singling out Gernet here is that even he who was one of the most important advocates for a less "romanistic" approach to questions of Greek law[51] still accepted the

---

[48] The law is quoted in [Dem.] XLVI.23: κληροῦν δὲ τὸν ἄρχοντα κλήρων καὶ ἐπικλήρων, ὅσοι εἰσὶ μῆνες, πλὴν τοῦ σκιροφοριῶνος. ἀνεπίδικον δὲ κλῆρον μὴ ἔχειν. See n.26, above, for evidence pertaining to the ἐπιδικασία's being obligatory for those adopted by will.

[49] We may infer this from the fact that testators would sometimes keep secret the contents of their wills (see n.4, above, for references to the discussion).

[50] Gernet (1955, p.122) accepts Bruck's hypothesis (presented in Bruck: 1909, p.54 and pp.96sq.) and adds: "ajoutons que, dans le droit athénien du IVe siècle, l'adoption testamentaire se distingue de l'autre par le fait qu'elle ne confère pas la saisine: différence assez grave, et qui parait bien dénoncer un développement sécondaire de l'institution, laquelle n'aurait d'abord compris sous le nom de διαθήκη que l'adoption au sens propre, l'adoption «contractuelle»". He expresses his own view on p.146: the difference between a will and adoption *inter vivos* is that the latter "a lieu par une convention expresse qui met en présence deux parties et qui, comme telle, produit des effets immédiates et définitifs", as opposed to a will, which is a unilateral act.

[51] Gernet (1938) pp.261-292, see also Gernet (1955), p.1. Bruck was aware of the problem and criticised the work of Beauchet for "die ständige Subsumtion unter die

view that the difference between the two types of adoption was first and foremost one of substance (one was a contract, the other was not), rather than one of procedure. Furthermore, his article has inspired, directly or indirectly, most later work concerning wills and adoption, although his hypothesis has been somewhat modified over time.

There is no need to question the observation that a testamentary adoption as opposed to an adoption carried out *inter vivos* was considered incomplete at the death of the testator, and that it was for this reason that it did not confer the right of ἐμβάτευσις on the adoptee. What will be questioned here is the assumption that it was the unilateral nature of the Athenian will that rendered a further ratification by the People's Court necessary. There are quite a few examples of unilateral acts which were never the less considered valid in IV. century Athens. These are the wills drawn up by Athenians who had legitimate natural sons. They will be discussed in more detail below; what is relevant to the present discussion is the fact that these wills did not have to be ratified by any juridical instance in order for them to come into operation, although they were to all appearances unilateral acts just as much as the wills made by childless Athenians.[52]

Here a different explanation will be suggested: it has been argued above that the major procedural difference between testamentary adoption and adoption *inter vivos* was that the person adopted *inter vivos* was enrolled in the phratry and deme of the adopter while the latter was still alive. The enrolment of a son adopted by will only took place after the death of the testator. It may have been of crucial importance to the rights of a son adopted *inter vivos* to the inheritance left by his adoptive father that he had been enrolled in his adoptive father's phratry and deme in the adopter's lifetime.

This solution is controversial. Most scholars have denied any juridical importance to this part of the procedure of adoption[53], although they

---

römischen Kategorien"; nevertheless, he himself regarded the roman and modern juristic categories as indispensable analytical tools (1909, p.19sq.).

[52] Dem.XXVII.13: Οὗτος γὰρ εὐθὺς μετὰ τὸν τοῦ πατρὸς θάνατον ᾤκει τὴν οἰκίαν εἰσελθὼν κατὰ τὴν ἐκείνου διαθήκην... See also Dem.XXVIII.5.

[53] The legal importance of the enrolment in the phratry is denied explicitly by Beauchet (1897), vol.I, pp.353-355, vol.II, p.11 and pp.18sq. (but see Bruck: 1909, p.54, n.3), Gernet (1955), p. 138, Ruschenbusch (1962), p.309, and Harrison (1968), p.89. Lipsius (1905-15) does not comment upon it at all. However, in Lipsius' view, too, the ἐπιδικασία in connection with a testamentary adoption replaced the contractual relationship (beiderseitige Willenserklärung) which constituted an adoption *inter vivos*. Becker ascribes some legal importance to the enrolment in the phratry, but adds

realise that the enrolment of an adopted son in the deme of his adopted father had certain effects on the adopted son when exercising his rights as a citizen. The right to Athenian citizenship was inherited as well as property, and just as an adoption would alter the successional position of the adoptee, it would also change his identity as a citizen. All through the life of a male Athenian, his privileged position as a citizen was determined by the fact that his parents were Athenian citizens and that he was a member of his father's deme. By the adoption the adopted son was given a new political identity, in that his rights to citizenship were determined by the fact that he was now considered the son of his adoptive father, and he would exercise his rights as a member of his adoptive father's deme. For example, Leostratos, who tried in vain to be recognised as the adopted son of Archiades, got himself entered on the πίναξ ἐκκλησιαστικός of Archiades' deme, and he also tried to have θεωρικόν paid to him as a member of that deme rather than of Eleusis, which was the deme of his natural father[54]. So the enrolment of an adopted son in the deme of his adoptive father was, then, of demonstrable importance for his identity as an Athenian citizen. It is harder to demonstrate that it also had effect on his right to inherit, which is what will be attempted in this chapter.

In order to determine the legal effects of the enrolment of the adoptee in the phratry and deme of his adoptive father, we must return to the institution of posthumous adoption. It has been argued above that the posthumous adoption of Euboulides III consisted only in the enrolment of Euboulides in his grandfather's phratry. Euboulides was still a minor when claiming the inheritance of Hagnias; the speaker tells us that Euboulides' natural brother acted as his κύριος, when the ἐπιδικασία was opened[55]. An Athenian only acquired deme-membership when he had reached the age of 18[56]. Nonetheless, the speaker argues that Euboulides had a claim on Hagnias' inheritance *qua* legally adopted son of Hagnias' cousin. Furthermore, we know at least two examples of women having been adopted[57]. A woman never became member of a deme, so we

---

"Handelte es sich um die Adoption eines mündiges Erwachsenen, so ist also die Eintragung in die Phratrie überhaupt überflüssig" (p.306).
[54] [Dem.] XLIV.35sqq.
[55] [Dem.] XLIII.15.
[56] For a recent discussion of whether the candidate had to be 18 or whether enrolment would take place in his 18th year, that is at the age of 17, see M.Golden, (1979).
[57] Cat. nos.13 and 17.

cannot claim that it was enrolment of the adoptee in the adopter's deme which in itself constituted the procedure of adoption.

However, the Athenians let their minor sons be enrolled in their phratries[58], and it appears from a passage in Isaios III.73-79 that they would also, in some cases, present their daughters to their phrateres[59]. Is it, then, possible that it was the enrolment of the adoptee in the phratry of his adoptive father which was of decisive importance for the rights of the adopted son?

Now, it is still disputed whether all Athenian citizens were members of phratries in the IV. century. If one adheres to the theory that membership of a phratry was not obligatory for all Athenians, the answer to the question asked above must be a plain "No". It is hardly probable that the right to adopt an heir was restricted to those citizens who happened to be members of phratries, while adoption was denied to those who were not. But, as noted already in chapter 2, the tendency among scholars to assume that citizenship was conditional upon membership of a phratry has become stronger over the last decade[60], although evidence has yet to appear with which the dispute may be settled once and for all. On the other hand, the observation that naturalised citizens had to choose a phratry when wanting to exercise their rights as Athenian citizens is a very strong indication that phratry-membership was still obligatory in the IV. century[61]. The

---

[58] P.Oxy. XXXI.2538, col.II, lines 25-27: πρῶτον μὲν οὖν ὡς εἰσήγαγέ με εἰς τοὺς φράτερας ἔ[τ]η γεγονότα τρ[ία] ἢ τέτταρα μάρτυρας ὑμῖν παρέξομαι. Cf. Aristophanes, Frogs, v.417, And. I.126sq., Dem.LVII.54, Isaios VIII.19. Lambert (1986) discusses the evidence and concludes that the age of the child to be introduced was discretionary (p.135). Furthermore, he argues in favour of two ceremonies of enrolment, the second being in connection with the κούρειον, and that it was only this ceremony that was of legal significance. This is countered by the evidence of P.Oxy. XXXI.2538, Isaios VIII.19, and Dem.LVII.54: the speakers focused on the *early* introduction as being proof of their identity as Athenian citizens.

[59] This passage has been the object of a long controversy. Gould (1980: pp.40-42) argued against the introduction of women to the Athenian phratries and has been followed by Sealey (1987), pp.16-19. Gould claimed that only prospective ἐπίκληροι would be introduced by their fathers to the phratries. Even if Gould's suggestion is correct (and the evidence is far from conclusive), it does not cause problems in this context, since an adopted daughter would in any case be an ἐπίκληρος at her adoptive father's death. (This has been pointed out by Lambert (1986) pp.146sq.)

[60] See ch.2, n.10.

[61] Hansen (1986), p.74 *pace* M.Osborne (1981-83), vol.IV, p.182. Hedrick (1990) argues in favour of a strong link between demes and phratries (see esp. pp.84sq.), and that, in the case of the phratry of the Demotionidai, the deme of Dekeleia was actively involved in the scrutiny of adult members of the phratry. He further substantiates his claim by providing evidence for the phratries' being local groups rather than kinship-groups (1991).

argumentation in the following paragraphs rests on the assumption that all Athenian citizens were members of phratries.

An attempt will be made to show that an heir who had been posthumously adopted was in a different legal position from the intestate heir who chose to remain in the οἶκος of his natural father. The procedure of posthumous adoption consisted *solely* in the adoptee's being admitted to the phratry and, if he was an adult, to the deme of his adoptive father as his son. Therefore, if it can be demonstrated that the adoption had any effect on his legal standing as compared to that of the collateral heirs of the deceased, this will prove, at the same time, the juridical importance of enrolment in phratry and deme.

1) A collateral heir who had had the inheritance awarded to him by ἐπιδικασία on the basis of being the closest relative of the deceased was entitled to take possession of the inheritance, but he could never be sure that he would keep it. If another claimant turned up, maintaining that he had a better claim than the heir in possession, the inheritance-case could be reopened. It was possible for other claimants to come forward up to five years after the death of the heir to whom the inheritance had been awarded in the first place[62].

Now, there is one known inheritance-case which strongly indicates that an intestate heir was in a position to bar further inheritance-suits instigated by other claimants, provided that he had been adopted posthumously into the οἶκος of the deceased. This is the case of Leochares who had been adopted posthumously into the οἶκος of his great-great-grandmother's brother. This posthumous adoption was attacked by means of a δίκη ψευδομαρτυρίων rather than by ἐπιδικασία[63].

Leochares had met the claim of his opponents with a διαμαρτυρία, stating that the inheritance was not to be the object of an inheritance-suit, since the deceased, Archiades, had left a γνήσιος υἱός, namely

---

[62] The law is quoted in [Dem.] XLIII.16: 'Ἐὰν δ' ἐπιδεδικασμένου ἀμφισβητῇ τοῦ κλήρου ἢ τῆς ἐπικλήρου, προσκαλείσθω τὸν ἐπιδεδικασμένον πρὸς τὸν ἄρχοντα, καθάπερ ἐπὶ τῶν ἄλλων δικῶν· παρακαταβολὰς δ' εἶναι τῷ ἀμφισβητοῦντι. ἐὰν δὲ μὴ προσκαλεσάμενος ἐπιδικάσηται, ἀτελὴς ἡ ἐπιδικασία τοῦ κλήρου. ἐὰν δὲ μὴ ζῇ ὁ ἐπιδικασάμενος τοῦ κλήρου, προσκαλείσθω κατὰ ταὐτά, ᾧ <ἂν> ἡ προθεσμία μήπω ἐξήκῃ. τὴν ἀμφισβήτησιν εἶναι τῷ ἔχοντι, καθότι ἐπεδικάσατο οὗ ἂν ἔχῃ τὰ χρήματα. (Cf. Isaios IV.25). That the time-limit (ἡ προθεσμία) was five years is clear from Isaios III.58 (cf. the time-limit of five years that applied to cases against guardians, Dem.XXXVIII.17).
[63] [Dem.] XLIV.45: καὶ πρῶτον μὲν τὴν διαμαρτυρίαν ἀναγνώτω, καὶ σφόδρα τὸν νοῦν αὐτῇ προσέχετε· περὶ γὰρ ταύτης ἡ ψῆφος οἰσθήσεται νυνί. See also the fierce attack on the procedure of διαμαρτυρία itself made by the speaker in 57.sqq.

himself[64]. According to Leochares' opponent who delivered [Dem.] XLIV, Leochares' natural father, Leostratos, and, presumably, Leochares himself as well, had taken possession of the inheritance. The speaker and his father had tried to enter on the disputed estate prior to the opening of the inheritance-suit, but they had been ousted from it by Leochares and Leostratos[65]. Thus, Leochares had behaved as if he had the right of ἐμβάτευσις, firstly by taking possession of the inheritance without prior ἐπιδικασία, secondly, and this is perhaps more important, by preventing his opponents from instigating the ἐπιδικασία by means of a διαμαρτυρία, in which he stated that he was a legitimate descendant of Archiades.

Admittedly, [Dem.] XLIV is very difficult to use as a source for the institution of posthumous adoption: it is almost impossible to determine whether the speaker is right in claiming that the actions of Leochares and his father were illegal, and it is equally if not more difficult to make a qualified guess as to what would have been Leochares' version of the case. Only one thing is relatively certain as far as Leochares' version is concerned: he claimed that he was the adopted son of Archiades[66]. It is also reasonable to assume that he based his claim on the basis of a *posthumous* adoption. The probability that he would claim that his great-great-grandmother's brother had adopted him personally is rather small. So even if the speaker is right when he claims that the posthumous adoption of Leochares was illegal, it is reasonable to assume that a man who had been posthumously adopted had the option of barring all subsequent reopenings of the inheritance-suit by stating in a διαμαρτυρία that he was a descendant of the deceased. The fact that it was possible for a posthumously adopted son to employ the διαμαρτυρία explains why we do not know of any disputed posthumous adoption having been attacked by means of ἐπιδικασία while the adopted son was still alive.

2) We know that an adoption would change the identity of the adoptee so that he lost his right to inherit from his natural father and from his natural father's relatives[67]. By being adopted, he would acquire the right to inherit from his adoptive father and, presumably, from his adoptive father's relatives. In this he would differ from a collateral

---

[64] [Dem.] XLIV.29, 42sq., 46, 48sqq.
[65] [Dem.] XLIV.32-34.
[66] [Dem.] XLIV.6, 49, 51.
[67] See notes 45 and 46 above.

heir. At the ἐπιδικασία, the closest collateral heir of a childless deceased would have the right to the deceased's property awarded to him, but he would not acquire the right to inherit from the relatives of the deceased. He did not get a new identity by taking possession of the inheritance, and he kept, therefore, the same placing within his ἀγχιστεία. Children could inherit from their parents' relatives: an Athenian could, for example, claim the inheritance of his father's or mother's cousin and have it awarded to him, provided that this cousin did not have any closer relatives who advanced a better claim. But if he had the inheritance of, say, his father's cousin awarded to him, he would still not be entitled to inherit from any other relatives of the deceased, if he was not himself placed within their ἀγχιστεία. This may seem a rather too obvious point to make here, but it becomes relevant, if we return briefly to the case presented in [Dem.] XLIII. Euboulides III was the posthumously adopted son of Euboulides II. His adoptive father, Euboulides II, was allegedly a first cousin of Hagnias whose inheritance is the object of the present law-suit. Euboulides III was the grandson of Euboulides II and was as such not to be counted as a member of Hagnias' ἀγχιστεία[68]. But because of the posthumous adoption, Euboulides III could now claim that he had been moved up one generation[69]. He now counted as the son of Hagnias' cousin and thus as a member of Hagnias' ἀγχιστεία.

If it had been perfectly clear to all that a person who had been posthumously adopted did not acquire the right to inherit from his adoptive father's relatives, Euboulides III would have had no case. Of course, the case presented in [Dem.] XLIII must be handled with care when used as a basis for any generalizations. We can never be sure of how each Athenian jury would respond to each individual case resembling that of Euboulides III. But the case shows, at least, that a posthumous adoption *could* be construed and presented in an Athenian court as causing a change in the successional position of the adoptee,

---

[68] Isaios XI.11-13. As pointed out in note 32 above, Theopompos' interpretation of the law prescribing the order of intestate succession is disputed. However, when it came to the question of whether the descendants of "sons of cousins" were excluded from the ἀγχιστεία or not, Theopompos could not play upon the same linguistic ambiguity of the law as when he claimed that he and Hagnias were "sons of cousins".

[69] E.g. [Dem.] XLIII.15: ψηφισαμένων δὲ ταῦτα τῶν φρατέρων τῶν τουτουὶ Μακαρτάτου, υἱὸς ὢν Εὐβουλίδου ὁ παῖς οὑτοσὶ προσεκαλέσατο Μακαρτάτον τοῦ κλήρου τοῦ Ἁγνίου εἰς διαδικασίαν...

conferring on him the right to inherit from the relatives of his adoptive father.

In [Dem.] XLIII.15 there is further evidence that a posthumously adopted son would be in a different legal position from that of a collateral heir: the speaker tells us that Euboulides III had claimed the inheritance "naming his (natural) brother as his κύριος" (κύριον ἐπιγραψάμενος τὸν ἀδελφὸν τὸν ἑαυτοῦ). This also points to the conclusion that a posthumously adopted son severed his ties to his natural father, just as if he had been adopted *inter vivos* or by will[70].

It is thus hard to maintain that the enrolment of the adoptee in the adopter's phratry (and deme, if the person adopted was a grown-up male) was of no juridical importance for the rights of the adoptee. The procedure of posthumous adoption consisted solely in the phratry's and deme's recognition of the adoptee as son of the adopter; even so, this procedure had the same effects on the rights of the adopted son as an adoption *inter vivos* would have had.

For this reason it may be concluded that a person adopted by will was *initially* on the same footing as the collateral heirs of the deceased, because he had not yet been enrolled in the testator's phratry and deme at the testator's death. If the phratry's and deme's acceptance of the adoption was decisive for whether a person could call himself son of the deceased or not, then a person adopted by will would have been prevented from stating in a διαμαρτυρία that the testator had left a γνήσιος υἱός. He would thus not have the means of barring an ἐπιδικασία, since he was not yet considered a descendant of the deceased. The inheritance was at this point ἐπίδικος. It must be noted that the speakers of both Isaios II and VII make a distinction precisely between enrolment in phratry and deme and testamentary adoption[71].

An instructive case in this connection is, in fact, that of Thrasyllos, the adopted son of Apollodoros, who delivered Isaios VII. In the beginning of his speech, he claims that, being a lawfully adopted descendant of Apollodoros, the procedure of διαμαρτυρία was in fact open to him, but that he had decided not to employ it. We may ask why he

---

[70] Compare the argument of Theopompos in Isaios XI.45-49. He counters an alleged accusation made by his opponents: in order to avoid liturgies, Theopompos had arranged for his son, Makartatos II, to be posthumously adopted into the οἶκος of Makartatos I. By this means his own property and that of Makartatos II would be kept separate, another indication that a posthumous adoption would have the same effect as a testamentary adoption and an adoption *inter vivos*.
[71] Isaios II.14, VII.1.

preferred to defend his position as adoptee in an ἐπιδικασία rather than barring his opponent from advancing the claim of his wife. According to the speaker himself, it was because he knew that his audience, that is the judges, preferred him to state his claim in court rather than by means of a διαμαρτυρία, and because he had great confidence in the justice of his cause. We may of course accept his explanation at face value, but a more sceptical reading is perhaps appropriate here. The speaker may in fact have preferred not to employ the διαμαρτυρία, because his adoption had not been completed before the adoptant's death. In (27)-(28) we are told that Apollodoros had died *before* Thrasyllos had been enrolled in his deme as his adopted son. This irregularity may have rendered it very risky indeed for the speaker to claim in a διαμαρτυρία that Apollodoros' inheritance was not ἐπίδικος, the risk consisting in the deposit he would have to pay, which amounted to 10% of the inheritance[72]. He would have to weigh his chances of success against the danger that his opponent might be able to convince the judges in a δίκη ψευδομαρτυρίων that his attempt to pass himself off as a descendant was (at least) premature, considering that the adoption had not been completed by his adoptive father in the latter's lifetime.

However, once a will had been ratified by the People's Court, and the adoptee duly enrolled in the phratry and deme of the testator, the adopted son could employ the διαμαρτυρία and thus prevent other claimants from instigating a new ἐπιδικασία. In Isaios V we find an adoptee adopted by will who did exactly this[73]. Thus, after the completion of a testamentary adoption, the adoptee had apparently the same standing as a son who had been adopted *inter vivos*.

To sum up: it has been concluded that the main difference between the three types of adoption was one of procedure rather than of substance. The right of ἐμβάτευσις of an adoptee depended on whether he had been duly accepted and recognised as an adopted son by the adopter's phratry and deme. Therefore, the most important difference between an adoption which had been carried out *inter vivos* and a testamentary adoption was not that the former was a contract and the latter, being a unilateral act, was not. It was the fact that the adoption had not been completed before the death of the testator that was the reason why a son adopted by will had to advance his claim by means of an ἐπιδικασία as

---

[72] See chapter 2, n.73.
[73] Isaios V.16.

opposed to one who had been adopted *inter vivos*. He was not in the privileged position of a descendant until his adoption had been carried out and recognised by the adopter's phratry and deme; therefore, the inheritance left by the testator was ἐπίδικος at the point of his death.

It has also been concluded that a posthumous adoption did not have to be ratified by the Archon or by the People's court in order to be legally valid. The only persons who could legally be posthumously adopted were those who had already had the inheritance of the deceased awarded to them by the People's Court. The procedure of posthumous adoption consisted in the heir being enrolled in the phratry (and deme, if he was an adult) of the deceased. Posthumous adoption differed from testamentary adoption only by the fact that, in a testamentary adoption, the adoptive father had played an active part by stating his wish that an adoption take place and naming the person he wanted as his successor. In both cases the actual adoption took place in the adopter's phratry and deme, and in both cases the candidate would have had the inheritance awarded to him by the People's Court prior to his adoption.

Finally it has been argued that there is no reason to believe that the rights of the adoptees differed in any respect according to which procedure had been employed, once the adoptions had been completed. Adoptees adopted by will or posthumously could and did employ the procedure of διαμαρτυρία to prevent other claimants from instigating renewed ἐπιδικασίαι. All adopted sons had to sever their legal ties to their natural fathers, and all three types of adoption changed the identity of the adoptee, both regarding his position within his adoptive father's ἀγχιστεία, and as a citizen, since, as a result of the adoption, he would henceforth exercise his citizen-rights, not as the son of his natural father, but as the son of the adopter.

4. Annulment of adoption

In Dem. XLI.3-5 we are told that Polyeuktos' adoption of his brother-in-law, Leokrates, was annulled, because the two fell out with each other[74]. Leokrates was married to Polyeuktos' youngest daughter, Kleiokrateia, and Polyeuktos had his daughter's marriage dissolved. Unfortunately, we are not told by which procedure the adoption was

---

[74] Cat. no.2.

cancelled, only that Leokrates later sued Polyeuktos and Spoudias, Kleiokrateia's second husband, probably in order to recover his own property which he had brought with him.

This example may indicate that it was possible for an adoptive father to cancel an adoption *inter vivos*, if he so wished[75]. On the other hand, an important legal provision is referred to in Isaios VI.63 which points to the conclusion that this was not the case. Here we are told that, if an adopter begets a natural son after the adoption has been carried out, his adopted son will still be entitled to inherit an equal share of his property. Even though the adoption had lost its original purpose, namely providing the adopter with a replacement for a natural son, still the adoptee could not be deprived of the rights which the adoption had conferred on him. And this points to the conclusion that, ideally, the adopter was not free to cancel the adoption as he pleased. The case of Polyeuktos and Leokrates may be an exception to the rule; but we have no way of determining this with any certainty, particularly since the speaker of Dem. XLI is so uninformative as regards the way in which the adoption was annulled, and as regards the procedure by which Polyeuktos was later sued by the adoptee.

It has been discussed whether a testator could revoke his will without obtaining the consent of his beneficiary. Since we know that it was possible for an Athenian to draw up a will without even telling his beneficiary, the answer must be that he definitely could. A will often functioned as a kind of safety-precaution which could be revoked whenever the testator decided that it was no longer necessary. Most of the known testators had died in war or while travelling; presumably these men still had the hope of begetting natural sons, provided that they returned safe and sound from their expeditions. In Isaios VII we are told how Apollodoros drew up a will before going to war. After his return he had a natural son born to him, and he probably revoked his

---

[75] A procedure called ἀποκήρυξις existed with which a father could repudiate a natural son. We have no example of an adoptive father having used this procedure to cancel an adoption. If Harrison is right in assuming that it was a procedure which could be employed if a father conceived reasons to doubt his paternity only after his son had been introduced to his phratry, then the procedure would probably entail that his son lost his right to Athenian citizenship (Harrison: 1968, pp.75sqq., followed by MacDowell (1978), p.91). In that case, the procedure was hardly appropriate in connection with the annulment of an adoption. The adopted son must have been able to claim his citizen-rights on the basis of his having descended from his natural father, if his adoption was cancelled. In any case, the information regarding the procedure of ἀποκήρυξις is too scanty to allow any safe conclusions.

will on this occasion. In any case, the will was not produced after his death: instead, Apollodoros had adopted the son of his former beneficiary *inter vivos*. There is only a little evidence for how wills were normally annulled. In Isaios I.25 the speaker claims that a will could only be revoked if the testator destroyed the actual document, but in Isaios VI we are told that Euktemon revoked his will by stating, in the presence of witnesses, that his will was no longer to be considered valid[76].

An additional fact speaks in the favour of the assumption that wills were regarded primarily as safety-precautions which could be used by men who did *not* want to make irrevocable decisions as opposed to those men who adopted *inter vivos*: wills were meant to come into operation only on certain conditions, most importantly on condition of the testator's having died childless. We know of at least one testator who stated further provisions in his will, namely Hagnias, whose will is referred to in Isaios XI.8sq. Hagnias had named his niece as his heir in a will, but had added the provision that his uterine half-brother was to succeed to his property, if his niece died childless.

Furthermore, in [Dem.] XLVI.24 a law is quoted which contained a dispensation from the Solonic provision that only men with no natural sons were allowed to dispose freely of their property. The law-text runs as follows: "If a father of legitimate sons makes any dispositions, his will shall be valid, if his sons die before being two years past entering puberty". ("Ὅ τι ἂν γνησίων ὄντων υἱέων ὁ πατὴρ διαθῆται, ἐὰν ἀποθάνωσι οἱ υἱεῖς πρὶν ἐπὶ διετὲς ἡβᾶν, τὴν τοῦ πατρὸς διαθήκην κυρίαν εἶναι.) This law is another example of how the Athenian will was regarded primarily as a safety-precaution. A will of this kind would come into effect on the condition not only of the testator's death, but also the death of his sons while still minors. This law certainly did not apply to adoption *inter vivos* [77], since there was no such thing as a conditional adoption *inter vivos*. Once the adoptee had been enrolled in his adoptive father's phratry and deme, his rights were protected to such an extent that not even natural sons subsequently born to the adopter were supposed to challenge his position.

As for an adopted son, he was not allowed to return (ἐπανιέναι) to the οἶκος of his natural father, except on certain conditions. In Isaios VI.44

---

[76] Isaios VI.32.
[77] As has been pointed out by Ruschenbusch (1962), pp.307sq.

the speaker refers to a law which forbade an adopted son to return to his natural father's οἶκος, unless he left a natural, legitimate son of his own body who was to take his place as the adopted son in the οἶκος of the adopter. This law is referred to in other speeches, too, and Harpokration informs us that the law was written on Solon's 21st ἄξων[78].

We know of only three adopted sons who exercised their right to return, and the procedure by which the return took place cannot be reconstructed in detail. We are told in [Dem.] XLIV that an adopted son ceased to be a member of the deme of his adoptive father when he returned to the οἶκος of his natural father[79], but there is no information as to whether there was any procedure of readmission when he returned to the deme of his natural father. It may be assumed that he would also have to be readmitted to the phratry of his natural father, but, again, it is impossible to tell whether the readmission was a mere formality, or whether there was to be any reproduction of the rituals associated with the ordinary admission of a legitimate son.

It appears from [Dem.] XLIII.78 that Makartatos II, the adopted son of Makartatos I[80], had had one of his own sons adopted posthumously as the son of Makartatos I. We know that Makartatos must have returned to the οἶκος of his natural father, Theopompos, since he had inherited Theopompos' property at the time when [Dem.] XLIII was delivered[81]. It may be inferred from the terminology of the speaker that the procedure employed when an adoptee "left a legitimate son behind" was that of posthumous adoption. In (77) Makartatos II is said to have "introduced" his son to his adoptive father's οἶκος (the verb εἰσάγειν is used), and the verb εἰσποιεῖν is used twice in (77sq.). This probably meant that the son who was left behind was to be enrolled in the adopter's phratry and deme as his new adopted son. Although the adoptee was not transferred from one οἶκος to another, he did, nonetheless, acquire a new identity: instead of being the grandson of the adopter he now became his son.

The same procedure was employed by the adopted sons of Archiades according to the speaker who delivered [Dem.] XLIV. Archiades' οἶκος had been continued through three generations by three successive

---

[78] Isaios IX.33, X.11, [Dem.] XLIV.64 and 68, Antiphon Ἐπιτροπικῷ κατὰ Καλλιστράτου (frg. IV, Baiter & Sauppe, =Harpokration, Lex.228, lines 4-7).
[79] [Dem.] XLIV.21, 22, 26, 28, 34, 35, 39, 44, 46, 52.
[80] Cat. no.23.
[81] [Dem.] XLIII.77sq. It is possible that Makartatos II still acted as the guardian of his natural son, since, in (77), the speaker accuses him of controlling two οἶκοι.

adoptees. Leokrates I who had first been adopted by Archiades left his legitimate son, Leostratos, in Archiades' οἶκος and returned to the οἶκος of his natural father. Later Leostratos did the same, leaving behind one of his sons, Leokrates II. In (22) the speaker alleges that this was in fact illegal[82], but he keeps contradicting himself on this point throughout the speech[83], and there is little reason to doubt that, technically, his opponents had acted in accordance with the letter of the law.

But when Leokrates II had died childless, his natural father, Leostratos, got his other son, Leochares, adopted as the son of Archiades. Prior to this adoption, Leostratos himself had made an attempt to return to the οἶκος of Archiades, but failed. In both cases Archiades' deme was involved in the adoptions: in the case of Leostratos, the deme-members refused to vote on his admission[84], whereas Leochares was enrolled in both Archiades' phratry and deme[85] as his fourth adopted son. The law providing for the return of an adoptee to the οἶκος of his natural father only permitted the adoptee to pass on his adoption to one of his direct descendants. According to the speaker of [Dem.] XLIV, Leochares had taken the place of his natural brother, and the speaker emphasises the fact that Leokrates II had died childless so that there were no descendants left to continue Archiades' line[86]. A parallel example to this way of interpreting the law very literally is found in Isaios X.11. Here, the speaker claims that an adopted son was only allowed to continue the οἶκος of his natural father if he *himself* returned: he was not allowed to let one of his own sons be posthumously adopted so as to return instead of himself. In fact, this interpretation of the law is in accordance with the way that posthumous adoptions were supposed to work, in that only heirs who had had the inheritance awarded to them were eligible for posthumous adoption. The male descendants of a man who had been adopted had no legitimate claim on the inheritance left by their *natural* grandfather, and were therefore not to be posthumously adopted into his οἶκος.

S.C.Humphreys is probably right when pointing out that technical legal rules such as the one dealt with here "often ran contrary to

---

[82] ...καὶ διὰ τριῶν σωμάτων κυρίαν τὴν ἐξ ἀρχῆς ποίησιν παρὰ τοὺς νόμους καταστήσας.
[83] E.g. [Dem.] XLIV.63 and 68.
[84] [Dem.] XLIV.40.
[85] [Dem.] XLIV.41.
[86] [Dem.] XLIV.24, 44, 47-48, 63-64, 68.

patterns of affection and association within the family"[87], for which she adduces the cases described in Isaios X and [Dem.] XLIV as evidence. She makes the observation that the Athenians sometimes tried to circumvent the law which prescribed that an adoptee was to sever his legal ties to his natural father.

On the other hand, it appears from [Dem.] LVIII.30-32 that this provision was taken very seriously indeed by the Athenians. According to the speaker, his father had moved a decree granting dining-rights in the Prytaneion to Charidemos *qua* son of Ischomachos. But Charidemos had been adopted by Aischylos[88], and would therefore not be entitled to receive honours bestowed on him because of his natural father. The speaker's father was prosecuted in a γραφὴ παρανόμων by Theokrines, allegedly on the grounds that the adoption of Charidemos would be invalid, if the decree was allowed to stand, and that, as a result of this, Charidemos would lose the property left by his adoptive father. Although the speaker claims that Theokrines' allegation was not true[89], it is worth noting that the result of the γραφὴ παρανόμων was that his father was fined the enormous sum of ten talents which led to his incurring ἀτιμία as a public debtor[90].

This case testifies to the difficulties which might arise when the concept of a natural father-son relationship conflicted with the rules pertaining to adoption. No doubt, the law which permitted an adoptee to return to the οἶκος of his natural father met some of these difficulties, for example in those cases where the οἶκος of an adoptee's natural father became empty after the adoption had been carried out[91]. In those cases, the problem of conflicting loyalties on the part of the adoptee was solved in that he was allowed to return; but at the same time the provisions of the law ensured that the family-line of the adopter would

---

[87] (1983b), p.7.
[88] Cat. no.34.
[89] "οὐδενὶ γὰρ πώποτε, ὦ ἄνδρες δικασταί, τοῦτο τῶν εἰσποιηθέντων συνέβη." (31)
[90] A Charidemos Aischylou is known from IG II.2 417, which is dated by Kirchner to the period after 330. Davies (1971) identifies him (p.7) with the Charidemos referred to in [Dem.] LVIII. The γραφὴ παρανόμων is dated to the years between 350 and 340 by Hansen (1974) p.35. Then, if Davies' identification is correct, we may infer that Charidemos remained in the οἶκος of his adoptive father for at least ten years after the decree had been pronounced illegal.
[91] This was probably what happened in the case of Makartatos II. In Isaios XI.49 we are told that Theopompos had two sons, and that he got one of them posthumously adopted into the οἶκος of Makartatos I. In [Dem.] XLIII Makartatos II has returned to the οἶκος of Theopompos, and it is clear from the speech that he was Theopompos' sole heir, which means that his brother had probably died by then.

also be continued in that it compelled the adoptee to leave a legitimate son behind who was to take his place.

Chapter 4: Why did the Athenians adopt?

In the forensic speeches, the adopter's reasons for adopting an heir are often placed centrally in the argumentation. No doubt, this apparent emphasis on the adopters' motives is partly due to the provision in the Solonic law which required that an Athenian who wanted to dispose legally of his property be of sound mind and free of any undue pressure from his surroundings. This provision seems to have been frequently employed as the legal foundation of attacks directed at adopted sons. The argumentation of Isaios II, for example, is centred on the question of whether the adopter, Menekles, had been under the influence of his ex-wife when he decided to adopt her brother. This would render the adoption invalid according to the law. Admittedly, the sceptical reader may claim that a speaker would sometimes focus deliberately on uncontroversial points, or on those points made by his opponent which could easily be refuted, while passing over in silence the arguments which might prove to be damaging to his cause. But in *Ath. Pol.* 35.2 we are told that in order to reduce the number of inheritance-suits the Thirty Tyrants revised the Solonic law by removing "the troublesome addition 'if not affected by madness, senility, or persuaded by a woman', so that there would be no opportunity for the sykophants." (...τὰς δὲ προσούσας δυσκολίας, ' ἐὰν μὴ μανιῶν ἢ γήρων ἢ γυναικὶ πιθόμενος' ἀφεῖλον ὅπως μὴ ᾖ τοῖς συκοφάνταις ἔφοδος). At least to the Thirty Tyrants, this clause appeared to have given rise to excessive litigation. Furthermore, bearing in mind the many allusions which are made to this clause in Isaios' speeches[1], it was probably no coincidence that the author of the *Ath. Pol.* chose to single out this particular revision made by the Thirty Tyrants in order to illustrate his point to his readers. The existence of such a provision would have rendered it of great importance to an adopted son to demonstrate that his adoptive father had had legal and plausible motives for adopting, when he was defending his adoption in court.

Some of the factors that might prompt a childless man to adopt an heir are described in Isaios II and VII. There is, however, reason to be cautious when treating these two speeches as evidence, since both were

---

[1] Isaios I.11, 20sq., 43, II.1, 14sq., 25, 38, IV.14sq., VI.9sq., VII.1, IX.37.

delivered by adopted sons in defence of their adoptions against attacks from the intestate heirs of their adoptive fathers. Thus, there is a risk that facts, and not least the adopters' motives for adopting, have been misrepresented by the speakers.

On the other hand, we may safely assume that the adopters' reasons for adopting, as represented in these speeches, were such as the audience would have considered acceptable and appropriate. An adopted son would have to represent the adopter's motives as conforming to the generally recognised reasons for adopting. In other words, it is of little importance even if the adoptions described in Isaios II and VII are closer to the Athenian idea of a model adoption than to the real events which preceded the individual law-suits. For while the two speeches must be handled with great care if used as evidence for the specific cases they describe, they may be used as reliable evidence for what "the ordinary Athenian" (represented by the judges in the People's Court) considered appropriate reasons for adopting an heir.

Bearing in mind these reservations, a passage from Isaios II.10 may be taken as a convenient starting-point for the discussion in this chapter. Here the adopted son of Menekles describes Menekles' reasons for adopting him thus: "after this event [Menekles' divorce], some time passed; then Menekles began to consider how to avoid being childless, and how to have someone who would look after him in his old age while he was alive, and, when he was dead, would bury him and, in the future, perform the rites for him [at his tomb]." (Μετὰ δὲ ταῦτα χρόνου διαγενομένου ἐσκόπει ὁ Μενεκλῆς ὅπως μὴ ἔσοιτο ἄπαις, ἀλλ' ἔσοιτο αὐτῷ ὅστις ζῶντά τε γηροτροφήσοι καὶ τελευτήσαντα θάψοι αὐτὸν καὶ εἰς τὸν ἔπειτα χρόνον τὰ νομιζόμενα αὐτῷ ποιήσοι.) According to the speaker, then, his adoptive father had three main reasons for adopting: he wanted to be supported in his old age and to be properly buried, and he wanted someone to attend to his tomb-cult. The aspect of γηροτροφία will be treated in the first section of this chapter, followed by a section dealing with the two other aspects, burial rites and the private tomb-cult together, primarily from a legal point of view. A final section will deal with yet another aspect which is not touched upon by Menekles' adopted son in the passage quoted above, namely to what extent the Athenians used adoption as a means of disrupting the order of intestate succession.

1. γηροτροφία

When discussing what may have prompted an Athenian to adopt an heir, the aspect of γηροτροφία has been the least difficult for modern readers to understand, as pointed out in the introduction. It is well known that a grown-up son was the only real security that an Athenian would have for being provided for in his old age. The dependence of aged parents on their children is a frequent theme in Greek literature[2]. A son was expected to provide for his parents' needs when his father had become too old to earn his own living, and he was even under a legal obligation to do so: if he failed in his duty, and if a γραφὴ κακώσεως γονέων was brought against him, he was punished with total ἀτιμία if convicted[3].

It is hard to tell to what extent a childless Athenian could count on his collateral relatives to support him. Whereas the obligations of sons towards their parents are often stressed in the forensic speeches along with, for example, the moral and legal obligations of male relatives to take care of poor ἐπίκληροι, the neglect of the needs of an aged uncle or aunt is almost absent from the list of rhetorical commonplaces of abuse. An exception is the passage in Aisch. I.102-104, where Timarchos is accused of having abandoned his old, blind uncle, Arignotos, to his fate after having cheated him out of his share of the family estate, which Arignotos had held jointly with Timarchos' father. But here, as in e.g. [Dem.] XLV.70, the message is rather that it is shameful to cheat or actively harm one's kinsfolk; the abuse does not rest on the fact that the speakers' opponents had simply failed to support their aged relatives financially.

Whatever the moral obligations of a nephew or cousin may have been (and it must be noted that there may have been great differences between individual instances), it can in any case be inferred from the argument in Isaios I.39sq. that the collateral relatives of a childless Athenian were not under any *legal* obligation to provide for his needs: "And if Kleonymos' [the testator's] father, Polyarchos, our grandfather,

---

[2] See the collection of evidence in Richardson (1933) pp.48-58 and in her catalogue of vase-paintings, and see further Hubbard (1989), Hunter (1990)

[3] And. I.74, Dem. XXIV.60, 103-107. In Isaios I.39 and VIII.32 it is claimed that grandchildren were under the same legal obligation to provide for their grandparents. For total ἀτιμία being inflicted on those convicted in a γραφὴ κακώσεως γονέων see further Hansen (1973) pp.94sq. In Dem.XXIV.60 οἱ τοὺς γονέας κακοῦντες are listed along with traitors and murderers as examples of the worst possible criminals.

happened to be alive and in need of provisions, or if Kleonymos had died leaving daughters unprovided for, we would be forced, for reasons of kinship, both to provide for our grandfather in his old age and to marry Kleonymos' daughters ourselves or to provide them with a dowry and marry them to others. And both our kinship and the laws and our sense of decency in regard to you would force us to do this, or else to incur the severest punishments and the deepest disgrace". (Καὶ εἰ μὲν Πολύαρχος ὁ πατὴρ ὁ Κλεωνύμου, πάππος δ' ἡμέτερος, ζῶν ἐτύγχανε καὶ τῶν ἐπιτηδείων ἐνδεὴς ὤν, ἢ Κλεώνυμος ἐτελεύτησε θυγατέρας ἀπορουμένας καταλιπών, ἡμεῖς ἂν διὰ τὴν ἀγχιστείαν καὶ τὸν πάππον γηροτροφεῖν ἠναγκαζόμεθα καὶ τὰς Κλεωνύμου θυγατέρας ἢ λαβεῖν αὐτοὶ γυναῖκας ἢ προῖκα ἐπιδιδόντες ἑτέροις ἐκδιδόναι, καὶ ταῦθ' ἡμᾶς καὶ ἡ συγγένεια καὶ οἱ νόμοι καὶ ἡ παρ' ὑμῶν αἰσχύνη ποιεῖν ἠνάγκαζεν ἄν, ἢ ταῖς μεγίσταις ζημίαις καὶ τοῖς ἐσχάτοις ὀνείδεσι περιπεσεῖν). The speaker's point is that, since his family-tie with Kleonymos implied that he had certain financial and social obligations to Kleonymos' father and daughters, it would not be fair to deprive him of Kleonymos' inheritance. Now, if the speaker could have demonstrated that he would have had a legal obligation to provide for *Kleonymos'* needs as well, this would obviously have strengthened his argument (cf. Isaios VIII.32)[4]. The fact that he does not claim that this was the case, but instead stresses his (hypothetical) obligation to provide for Kleonymos' father who was also his own grandfather and his (hypothetical) obligations to his daughters (who would have been ἐπίκληροι) points to the conclusion that collaterals were not under any legal obligation to take care of their aged and childless relatives.

In his book *Lending and Borrowing in Ancient Athens*, P. Millett has argued for a crucial difference between a father-son relationship and other relationships based on kinship, namely that it was a constituent feature of the former that sons owed perpetual χάρις to their parents[5]. A son's obligation to render constant support to his parents could therefore not be questioned, except under those circumstances where a father had himself released his son from his obligations by depriving

---

[4] That it is the speaker's intention to stress the reciprocity of the testator's and his own family-relationship is very clear from his concluding remark in I.47: ὥσθ' ἡμᾶς μὲν ἐν ἀμφοτέροις, ὦ ἄνδρες, καὶ ἐν τῷ δοῦναι καὶ ἐν τῷ λαβεῖν οἰκείους ὄντας εὑρήσετε, τούτους δὲ νῦν μὲν ἀναισχυντοῦντας καὶ τὴν οἰκειότητα καὶ τὴν ἀγχιστείαν λέγοντας, ὅτι λήψεσθαί τι προσδοκῶσιν. ἐν δὲ τῷ δοῦναι πολλοὺς ἂν καὶ συγγενεῖς καὶ φίλους ἐκείνου προείλοντο οἰκειοτέρους.
[5] pp.127-139.

him of his rights to become an active citizen[6]. For in doing this (e.g. by hiring his son out as a prostitute) a father would effectively remove one of the most fundamental reasons for his son's debt of χάρις: his having been born, recognised, and brought up as a prospective Athenian citizen[7]. However, other relationships based on kinship did not comprise this feature of a built-in debt of χάρις: they were thus not asymmetrical in their nature, but rather depended on the parties maintaining a constantly balanced reciprocity[8].

When seen in this light, the establishment by means of adoption of a fictive father-son relationship with all its implications becomes extremely important as a social institution: the plight of old age, especially when combined with poverty, may well have been accentuated by the fact that it may have been impossible for an old, childless person to keep up a balanced relationship with his relatives, being unable to reciprocate[9].

So it would seem that for a childless Athenian the safest way of ensuring γηροτροφία for himself would be to adopt a son. The aspect of γηροτροφία would of course have been relevant almost exclusively to adoption *inter vivos*. As noted above, it is clear from the description given by Menekles' adopted son of his own adoption that ideally an adoption *inter vivos* should be a faithful imitation of a biological father-son relationship, even on an emotional level[10]. That the Athenians were indeed aware of the gap between ideal and reality in this respect is of less importance here[11]. The point is that adoption *inter vivos* was the

---

[6] See e.g. Aisch. I.13sq.
[7] The notion of children being indebted to their parents for having been born and brought up is expressed in Lyk. *Leokr.* 94. That "treating one's parents well" formed an important part of the duties of an Athenian citizen *qua* citizen is clear from what Aischines reports on the δοκιμασία ῥητόρων, I.28. Cf. *Ath.Pol.* 55.3 and Dem.LVII.70 on the δοκιμασία of archons.(It is also significant that the punishment inflicted on a person who had been convicted in a γραφὴ κακώσεως γονέων was ἀτιμία, and not a fine; that is, a verdict would affect the culprit's rights to actively exercise his citizenship.)
[8] Millett (1991), p.135sq.
[9] Cf. Men.'Αδελφοί β' fr. 6 (ed. Körte, Bibl.Teubneriana 1953): ἔργον εὑρεῖν συγγενῆ πένητός ἐστιν· οὐδὲ εἷς γὰρ ὁμολογεῖ αὑτῷ προσήκειν τὸν βοηθείας τινὸς δεόμενον, αἰτεῖσθαι γὰρ ἅμα τι προσδοκᾷ.
[10] κἀκεῖνός τε τὴν πρόνοιαν εἶχεν ὥσπερ εἰκός ἐστι πατέρα περὶ ὑέος ἔχειν, καὶ ἐγὼ τὸν αὐτὸν τρόπον ὥσπερ γόνῳ ὄντα πατέρα ἐμαυτοῦ ἐθεράπευόν τε καὶ ᾐσχυνόμην, καὶ ἐγὼ καὶ ἡ γυνὴ ἡ ἐμή, ὥστ' ἐκεῖνον πρὸς τοὺς δημότας ἐπαινεῖν ἅπαντας.
In Isaios II.13 the speaker stresses the emotional aspect of adoption (it is "a refuge from loneliness" and "a consolation of life for childless people") when stating the lawgiver's reasons for passing his law.
[11] See e.g. Lyk.*Leokr.* 48: ὥσπερ γὰρ πρὸς τοὺς φύσει γεννήσαντας καὶ τοὺς ποιητοὺς τῶν πατέρων οὐχ ὁμοίως ἔχουσιν ἅπαντες ταῖς εὐνοίαις, οὕτω καὶ πρὸς τὰς

only one of the three types to even *attempt* this imitation. Although a son adopted by will or by posthumous adoption was expected to take the place of a natural son in regard to his deceased adoptive father, and although these types of adoption also involved a reproduction of the ceremonies of affiliation in phratry and deme, the whole emotional and personal dimension was absent from a father-son relationship established by testamentary or posthumous adoption. There is a world of difference between the (allegedly) close relationship between Menekles and his adopted son that lasted for 23 years after the adoption[12] and that of, say, Euboulides III and his father by posthumous adoption, Euboulides II, whom he had never even known[13].

Of course, it was recognised that a testator would usually choose an heir because of already existing ties of friendship or kinship - and conversely that a testator would never choose an heir to whom he was indifferent or hostile (this constitutes an important part of the argument in Isaios I, IV, and IX). But the personal and emotional relationship of φιλία or συγγένεια between testator and beneficiary was not turned into or formally reclassified as a father-son relationship in the testator's lifetime. Both legally and socially, a person who had been chosen as a beneficiary in a will was no more and no less obliged to provide for the testator's needs in the latter's life-time than any other friend or relative.

Although it cannot be ruled out completely that testators might sometimes have used their wills to put social pressure on their prospective heirs, this would have required that the testators had made publicly known the contents of their wills, and at least that they had revealed it to their beneficiaries. Since wills are often referred to as more or less secret transactions[14], and since we never hear of any testators who had made use of their wills in this way, it can be safely concluded that the aspect of γηροτροφία played only a minor rôle, if any, in connection with testamentary adoptions.

No doubt, this is one of the reasons why adoption *inter vivos* could sometimes be construed as a more "true" adoption than testamentary adoption in some of the lawcourt speeches. Not only did the rites of affiliation in phratry and deme alter the juridical standing of an adoptee

---

χώρας τὰς μὴ φύσει προσηκούσας, ἀλλ' ὕστερον ἐπικτήτους γενομένας καταδεέστερον διακεῖνται.
[12] Isaios II.15, 45.
[13] Cat.no.24.
[14] Isaios IV.13, VII.1sq. and [Dem.] XLVI.28.

in regard to his adoptive father's inheritance, making his estate ἀνεπίδικος[15], they also formally imposed the duties of a natural son along with a son's debt of χάρις on the adoptee. This would have had the most visible and wide-ranging effects in connection with adoption *inter vivos*.

2. The private tomb-cult and Athenian οἶκοι

Menekles' reasons for adopting a son (as represented by the adoptee himself) were quoted in the beginning of this chapter to illustrate that the generally accepted motives for adopting were at least threefold: Menekles wanted to be looked after in his old age, to be properly buried, and to have the proper rites (τὰ νομιζόμενα) carried out at his tomb[16]. Now, Menekles had adopted a son *inter vivos*, and, as pointed out in the previous section, it was only in connection with this type of adoption that the aspect of γηροτροφία was important as an incentive for adopting an heir. If we apply the speaker's representation to testamentary and posthumous adoption, we are left with concern for the funeral and the annual commemorative rites (which apparently depended on the continuation of the adopter's οἶκος) as the most important reason for carrying out those adoptions that would only take effect after the death of the adopter.

Traditionally, a strong link has been recognised by modern scholars between the institution of adoption on the one hand and Athenian private tomb-cult and the concept of οἶκος on the other. In this respect, Fustel de Coulanges' book *The Ancient City* (1864) has had a considerable impact on subsequent research on Athenian adoption[17]. His claim that, in the archaic period, the rights of the individual were not recognised, that land was owned collectively by the *genos*, and that the head of an οἶκος was seen just as a temporary 'custodian' of the family property and its sacra has been remarkably strong-lived. According to this view, the

---

[15] See ch.3, section 3, above.
[16] Isaios II.10. In Isaios VII.30-32, the latter aspect is closely linked with the adopter's desire of preventing his οἶκος from "becoming empty", a concern which is not explicitly ascribed to Menekles in Isaios II. But the speaker does point out that Menekles' οἶκος' becoming empty will be the direct result of his opponent's winning the case (II.35-37, 43).
[17] See the detailed survey of the history of the modern invention of the *genos* as an archetype in Bourriot (1976) vol.I, pp.42-198.

tomb-cult remained an important manifestation of the family that comprised not only the living but also the dead, even when the balance of power was shifted from the *gene* to the πόλις in the classical period. The family was still conceptualised diachronically as stretching back into the mists of time and as having to be continued indefinitely through future generations. In the classical period, this diachronic family-concept still survived, but now it was the πόλις that took an active interest in securing the continuation of the family-lines of its citizens, both for fiscal and for religious reasons[18].

But over the last decades scholars have shown an increasingly critical attitude to his work[19]. In their preface to the 1980 edition, S.C. Humphreys and A. Momigliano have pointed out the grave inconsistencies in Fustel de Coulanges' fundamental hypothesis, and, furthermore, they have demonstrated how his work bore a contemporary (nineteenth century) political message. More importantly, S.C. Humphreys (1980b) has demonstrated on the basis of archaeological evidence that it was highly unlikely that an Athenian would be commemorated through more than two generations of descendants[20].

Now, if the conventional view of the Athenian family has to be rejected in part as a nineteenth century invention, we are still left with the topoi in the inheritance-speeches that stress the importance of adoption as a means of preventing an οἶκος from becoming ἔρημος[21], along with arguments concerning rites of burial and annual commemoration of the deceased[22]. They cannot just be dismissed as irrelevant or as anachronistic survivals from an earlier period. In the argumentation of some of the speeches, they occupy a far too central

---

[18] Beauchet (1897) vol. II, Glotz (1904) 347sq., Bruck (1909), Lipsius (1905-15) pp. 58, 508sq. and 574sq., Wolff (1944) p.50, 93sqq., Gernet (1955), Jones (1956), Brindesi (1961), Lacey (1968); see also Schaps (1979) p.32.

[19] See e.g. Bourriot (1976). See also MacDowell (1989) who argues that, at least as early as the time of Solon, Athenian citizens were recognised as independent individuals rather than as members of family-corporations, and that the use of the word οἶκος to denote larger kinship-groups is a later (V. century) phenomenon. Hedrick (1991) presents strong arguments against the conventional notion of phratries originating as powerful kinship-groups.

[20] Cf. Humphreys (1981) pp.270sq. and Garland (1985) pp.106sq.

[21] See e.g. Isaios VII.30sqq. and [Dem.] XLIII.77sq.

[22] The most important passages found in speeches on inheritance are Isaios I.10, II.36sq. and 45sqq., IV.19 and 26, VI.39sqq., VIII.21-27 and 38sq., IX.4 and 32, [Dem.] XLIII.11sqq. and 78sqq., [Dem.] XLIV.32sq., [Dem.] XLVIII.12.

position for them not to reflect contemporary values of the IV. century[23].

It is beyond doubt that a natural son had strong obligations to provide a proper funeral for his parents and to take care of the annual commemorative rites at their tomb. Neglecting the tomb of one's parents could be represented as a way of maltreating them, analogous to the offence of neglecting their needs while they were still alive[24].

However, before it can be decided to what extent the desire to obtain a proper burial and annual commemorative rites could motivate a childless Athenian to adopt an heir, it is necessary to look into the obligations incumbent on the *collateral* relatives of a childless man. For it is quite clear from the inheritance speeches that collateral heirs did have certain religious obligations towards their deceased childless relatives. If it turns out that the difference between their obligations and those of a son was minimal, then we must reconsider the religious arguments presented by adoptive sons in their lawcourt speeches.

In Isaios II, Menekles' adopted son represents his obligations to his adoptive father after the latter's death as twofold: he had to provide a proper funeral for him (36sq.), and to carry out the annual rites at his tomb in the future (46sq.). In his reference to the funeral he mentioned the rites that were carried out on the third and ninth day along with the actual burial[25]. The rites that were carried out during the thirty days of mourning following the actual death were designated τὰ νομιζόμενα[26] or τὰ νόμιμα[27], and thus were not distinguished terminologically from the annual rites of commemoration, except when referred to separately as τὰ τρίτα and τὰ ἔνατα[28]. Even so, it is important to keep in mind the difference between the rites of passage and the annual rites of

---

[23] This has been recognised by Hardcastle (1980), pp.12-16 and W.E.Thompson (1981), cf. S.C.Humphreys (1983b) p.31.
[24] Lyk. *Leokr.* 147, Dem. XXIV.107, Xen.Mem.II.2,13. In Aisch.I.13 we are told that all sons had an obligation to bury their fathers and carry out the prescribed rites for them, even if they had been hired out as prostitutes when minors.
[25] Καὶ ὡς ἔθαψά τε ἐγὼ αὐτὸν καὶ τὰ τρίτα καὶ τὰ ἔνατα ἐποίησα καὶ τἆλλα τὰ περὶ τὴν ταφήν, τὰς μαρτυρίας ὑμῖν τῶν εἰδότων ἀναγνώσεται.
[26] E.g. Aisch. III.77, [Dem.] XLVIII.12, Isaios IV.19, IX.4; 32. For the period of mourning lasting thirty days, see Lysias I.14.
[27] E.g. Dein. II.8
[28] It is disputed when τὰ τρίτα were carried out. Kurtz and Boardman (1971) argue that the rites took place on the same day as the ἐκφορά (pp.144sqq.), which is accepted by Humphreys (1983b), p.86sq. The rites carried out on the thirtieth day, τὰ τριακόστια or αἱ τριακάδες are not known from any contemporary Athenian source, but figure in a decree from V. century Iulis (IG 12.593.20, τὰ τριακόστια) and in later lexicographers and commentators.

commemoration when comparing the obligations incumbent on collateral heirs to those of descendants. For while it is beyond doubt that collaterals were both morally and legally obliged to carry out the rites of passage during the period of mourning, the available evidence suggests that they had no responsibility for the rites that were to be carried out after this point.

In his important article "Γενεσία: a forgotten festival of the dead" Jacoby argued that the Athenian public festival on the 5th of Boedromion, the γενεσία, had been reserved by Solon for the yearly rites of commemoration at the tombs. Whatever Solon's reasons for introducing this public festival[29], the result was that each Athenian would be able to carry out the annual rites only at the tomb of his own immediate ascendants, unless all members of his family, including collaterals, were buried together at the same site[30]. This, in turn, means that whereas a collateral relative could be held responsible for the rites connected with the funeral of a childless deceased, he could not reasonably be expected to take care of his tomb-cult. In the following paragraphs it will be argued that this observation can be supported by the information found in the inheritance-speeches.

It appears from the law quoted in [Dem.] XLIII.58 that those in possession of an inheritance were responsible for the burial of the deceased (οἱ τὰ χρήματα ἔχοντες), and if the deceased left no property, his relatives (οἱ προσήκοντες) had to see to it[31]. We know of at least three instances where collateral relatives had taken it upon themselves to carry out the funeral of a childless deceased[32]. Furthermore, in five of Isaios' eleven speeches dealing with inheritance (II, IV, VI, VIII, and IX) the speakers refer to the funerals of the deceased in their narratives as an important part of their argumentation.

---

[29] Jacoby focused on the question of Solon's motives for establishing one fixed date for the festival, and his interpretation is largely based on what Bourriot has termed the "*genos*-archetype" (1976, vol. I, pp.71-94): Solon wanted to curb the power of the *gene*, and by breaking their monopoly of ancestor-worship, he could achieve his aim of "developing the clan state into a citizen's state" (1944, p.70).

[30] Humphreys (1983b), p.87. Jacoby did not state this explicitly.

[31] It must be noted, however, that the law does not aim at securing the proper rites of passage for the deceased: it merely aims at ensuring that the body is removed. Nor is it addressing the problems particular to childless Athenians: οἱ προσήκοντες applies to descendants as well as collaterals, and the law is aimed at dead metics and slaves as well as Athenian citizens. Humphreys (1983b, p.83) is probably right when she interprets it as a direct response to a situation of emergency as e.g. the plague of 430 (cf. Thukydides II.52).

[32] Isaios IV.26, VIII.38, [Dem.] XLVIII.12.

The most informative speeches in regard to the obligations of collateral relatives are Isaios IV, VIII, and IX[33]. Isaios IV and IX, however, were both delivered as attacks on wills providing for adoption, and it must be noted that the speakers' mentioning of the funerals may simply have been a means of demonstrating that their opponents had not lived up to their obligations as descendants.

It appears from the vivid description in Isaios VIII.21-27 that a prospective heir would be at an advantage when claiming an inheritance, if he had been responsible for the funeral of the deceased. Kiron, allegedly the speaker's maternal grandfather, had died intestate, and after his death his nephew[34] played a trick on Kiron's grandchildren which prevented them from taking charge of his funeral. The speaker relates this in great detail along with the story of how he took advice from the *exegetes* and covered all expenses of τὰ ἔνατα, "so that they [his opponents] would not be able to gain any advantage over me in this way by telling you in court that I had not contributed anything towards the costs of the funeral" (ὅπως δὲ μηδέν μου ταύτῃ πλεονεκτοῖεν, παρ' ὑμῖν φάσκοντες οὐδέν με εἰς τὴν ταφὴν ἀνηλωκέναι... (39)). A close parallel to the situation described in Isaios VIII is found in [Dem.] XLIV.32 where it is related how rival claimants had fought over who was to be in charge of the funeral of Archiades' posthumously adopted son[35]. In both these cases the problem was not so much having the deceased buried as deciding who had the right to carry out the funeral.

The perceived link between funerary obligations and rights to an inheritance is also found expressed in Isaios IV and IX. In Isaios IV.26 we are told by the *synegoros* of the collateral heirs that they had taken care of the funeral of their father's cousin. This they had done as a result of the negligence of their opponent, and the fact that the latter had not taken care of the funeral makes it "most impious" for him to advance his claim on the inheritance (πῶς οὐκ ἀνοσιώτατος εἴη, ὃς τῷ τεθνεῶτι μηδὲν τῶν νομιζομένων ποιήσας τῶν χρημάτων αὐτοῦ ἀξιοῖ; IV.19). However, it is clear from Isaios IX that it was not absolutely necessary for a claimant to have been actively involved in the funeral in order for

---

[33] Isaios II and VI are less relevant, since, in Isaios II, the funeral is recounted by a son who had been adopted *inter vivos*, and who simply wants to prove that he has lived up to his obligations as a *descendant* (cat. no.3); whereas in Isaios VI we find a number of people who all claimed to be descendants of the deceased and who all wanted to take charge of the funeral.

[34] Isaios VIII.31-33.

[35] Cat.no. 18. For the details of this case, see ch.3, section 3, above.

him to advance his claim in court: while the speaker blames his opponent for his negligence and greed[36], he has to admit that he himself had not buried him, either. Those in charge of the funeral had been the testator's friends and fellow soldiers[37], which did not prevent the speaker from claiming the inheritance. But it is worth noting that the speaker repeats no less than three times as an excuse that he had been abroad at the time of the funeral[38].

But while it is clear from the argumentation of the speeches that collateral relatives had strong moral obligations to carry out the funeral and the rites of passage during the thirty days of mourning, the evidence for their having any obligations after this point is at best ambiguous. In Isaios I.10 the speaker, a collateral heir, who is challenging a will in a διαδικασία, bases his argument on the assumption that a collateral heir could be expected to take care of the annual commemorative rites as well as the funeral: the deceased, Kleonymos, had decided to make a will, because he had fallen out with the guardian of his nephews, who were then still minors. The speaker continues: "he thought it would be terrible to leave his worst enemy as the guardian of his relatives and in charge of his possessions, and if this man, with whom he had been at variance while alive, was to carry out the rites for him, *until we came of age* " (ἡγεῖτο γὰρ δεινὸν εἶναι τὸν ἔχθιστον τῶν οἰκείων ἐπίτροπον καὶ κύριον τῶν αὑτοῦ καταλιπεῖν, καὶ ποιεῖν αὐτῷ τὰ νομιζόμενα τοῦτον, ἕως ἡμεῖς ἡβήσαιμεν, ᾧ ζῶν διάφορος ἦν.) It is clear that τὰ νομιζόμενα here means the annual commemorative rites as well as the funeral. If the speaker is right in assuming that collateral heirs could be counted on to take care of the annual rites, why would an Athenian want to adopt by will at all?

In fact, there is no parallel evidence to support the speaker in this assumption: what is even more curious is that the speaker does not utter a single word about his own intentions to take care of Kleonymos' tomb-cult after having had his inheritance awarded to him. His silence on this point becomes significant when we compare his speech to the other extant speeches on inheritance delivered by collateral relatives: Isaios III, IV, V, IX, X, and XI and [Dem.] XLIII, XLIV and XLVIII.

The speaker of [Dem.] XLIV is the only one who touches on this issue by suggesting that a son be adopted posthumously into the οἶκος of

---

[36] Isaios IX.32.
[37] Isaios IX.4.
[38] Isaios IX.3; 4; 7.

Archiades to replace the present adopted son Leochares[39]. This, of course, implies that there would be a descendant to take care of Archiades' tomb-cult. But none of the other speakers mention their own future obligations towards the deceased. Admittedly, a possible explanation of their utter silence on this topic may be that it was taken for granted by the audience that collaterals would naturally take care of the tomb-cult of a childless relative. But this explanation seems unlikely when we bear in mind that four of the eight speeches (Isaios IV, V, IX, and X) were delivered as attacks on adopted sons who would probably stress their own willingness to fulfill their religious obligations to their adoptive fathers along the lines of the speakers of Isaios II and VII. Why is it, then, that those speakers who contest the validity of adoptions hardly ever take pains to counter the arguments of their opponents by referring to their own obligations as collaterals, thus depriving their opponents of an important argument in favour of upholding their adoptions?

I would suggest, if only tentatively, that the reason for the silence of the collaterals was that they were not required or expected to take care of any rites beyond the close of the period of mourning. I would also suggest that they could afford to keep silent on this point, because such considerations were not seen as relevant to the case they were pleading.

An adopted son would always have to justify his position as a descendant in *general* terms, emphasising the special duties of a descendant as opposed to those of collateral relatives and stressing the reasons why his adoptive father had decided to adopt at all. As noted in the introduction, he would have to represent the motives of his adoptive father in such a way that they would appear both plausible and acceptable to his audience, and eulogizing the institution of adoption as such was an indispensable argument in this context. But the task of a collateral relative was quite different from that of an adoptee. Whereas the latter had to justify his adoption in general terms, a collateral heir who tried to have an adoption overruled could structure his argument in particular terms: he had to persuade the judges that either 1) the will was a fake (if the adoption was testamentary), or 2) the adoption was illegal (because the adopter had been out of his mind, persuaded by a woman, the procedure had been wrong, etc.), or 3) whether the adoption be a sham or not, the adoptee was in any case unworthy of his

---

[39] [Dem.] XLIV.43, 66.

position as a descendant (e.g. because he had neglected his religious duties towards the adoptee). The collateral relative would not have to dwell on the consequences of overruling the adoption, nor did he have to construct an attack on the instution as such; he only had to argue that this *particular* adoption was implausible or illegal and could not possibly be upheld.

The two different positions of collaterals and adoptees respectively call for two different types of rhetorical argument, and it was invariably the adoptee who was left with the burden of proof[40]. He would have to stress in general terms the importance of leaving a descendant behind so that the οἶκος of the adopter did not become empty and his tomb-cult neglected, and in particular terms that he himself was fully worthy of the position as a descendant.

To conclude: whereas a descendant was both morally and legally obliged to see to the annual commemorative rites at the tomb of his adoptive father, the obligations of collateral relatives did not extend beyond the period of mourning. This, in fact, ties up with the previous section on γηροτροφία: descendants were seen as being in a perpetual debt of χάρις to their parents, and their obligations to them went beyond the point of death and burial. Sons owed their identity as Athenian citizens to their immediate ascendants, and it appears from *Ath.Pol.* 55.3 that parental tomb-cult formed an important part of Athenian civic identity: in connection with the δοκιμασία of archons, the candidates had to state not only the identity of their parents and grandparents, but also the location of their tombs.

This did not apply to collateral relatives: once the funerary rites had been carried out, the relationship of "balanced reciprocity" between themselves and the deceased would terminate, unless they decided to provide a descendant for him by means of posthumous adoption. It will be argued in chapter 6 that an Athenian could by no means rely on his relatives to provide for such an adoption.

Thus, we do not necessarily have to operate with the idea of the Athenian individual family-lines having to be perpetuated indefinitely into the future in order for us to understand why it was a disaster to die childless, leaving one's οἶκος empty. It was only by continuing his

---

[40] The logic of "you can fake a will, but you cannot fake kinship" is clearly expressed in e.g. Isaios IV.15-17. Cf. the Aristotelian *Problemata* 950b.

family-line by leaving a descendant, natural or adopted, that an Athenian could be sure that he would receive due commemoration after his death.

3. Adoption and the order of intestate succession

Many scholars still assume that adopting an heir was the only way in which an Athenian could disrupt the order of intestate succession[41]. But on that assumption the οἶκος and tomb-cult motifs found in the foresic speeches must be handled with the utmost care by us when attempting to prove that such considerations were often, *in actual fact*, the main reason for adopting an heir. Passages are found in the forensic speeches in which it is alleged that strife within the adopter's family was often what prompted him to adopt, and one of these passages may be quoted here to serve as an example: "For you see that most people who adopt sons do so because they have been seduced by flattery and often because they engage eagerly in fighting against their relatives." (ὁρᾶτε γὰρ ὅτι ταῖς κολακείαις οἱ πλεῖστοι ψυχαγωγούμενοι καὶ ταῖς πρὸς τοὺς οἰκείους διαφοραῖς πολλάκις φιλονικοῦντες ποιητοὺς υἱεῖς ποιοῦνται. [Dem.] XLIV.63) Similar allegations made e.g. in Isaios I.10 and IV.18 may corroborate this statement. It must be emphasised, however, that these passages are all found in forensic speeches which were delivered as attacks on adoptions. In Isaios I, the speaker uses it as an argument that the will which is under attack was drawn up as a direct result of a family-strife. He claims that the will ought to be considered invalid, alluding to the clause in the Solonic law on wills which required that the testator be of sound mind when making his dispositions. The testator in question had made his will in anger, and he was, therefore, not "thinking straight" at the time (διέθετο δὲ ὀργισθεὶς καὶ οὐκ ὀρθῶς βουλευόμενος. Isaios I.43).

Indeed, in the three speeches which were delivered by or on behalf of adopted sons (Isaios II, VI, and VII, not counting [Dem.] XLIII which is

---

[41] Of more recent publications see e.g. Harrison, (1968), p.82 although he modifies this view in his chapter on wills, pp. 149sq., G.E.M.de Ste. Croix (1970), where he points out the inconsistency in Harrison's position, D.M.MacDowell, (1978)p. 101 and (1982), where it is implied that choosing someone as one's universal heir would necessarily involve adoption, R.Lane Fox, (1985).

dealing with a posthumous adoption), the good relationship between the adopters and their adoptees is emphasised; but only in one case do we find an adopted son referring to strife within the adopter's family as a direct cause of his being adopted. This is in Isaios VII in which Thrasyllos, the adopted son of Apollodoros, defends his adoption against an attack made by the daughter of Apollodoros' paternal uncle, Eupolis. Thrasyllos narrates how Apollodoros, having lost his father, was cheated by Eupolis, who acted as Apollodoros' guardian. The speaker's own grandfather who had married Apollodoros' mother brought up the orphaned Apollodoros as a member of his own household and later supported him in bringing two law-suits against Eupolis to recover his property[42]. The speaker concludes: "So many people, members of the jury, witnessed the adoption which took place both because of the old hostility felt by him (i.e. Apollodoros, the adopter) towards my opponents, and because of his kinship and strong friendship with us."
('Ἐπὶ μὲν τοσούτων μαρτύρων, ὦ ἄνδρες, γέγονεν ἡ ποίησις, ἔχθρας παλαιᾶς αὐτῷ πρὸς τούτους οὔσης, φιλίας δὲ πρὸς ἡμᾶς καὶ συγγενείας οὐ μικρᾶς ὑπαρχούσης. Isaios VII.29) Even so, the speaker found it necessary to modify this allegation in his very next sentence: "But I also think that I can easily show you that even if there had been no enmity between him and my opponents, nor friendship between him and us, Apollodoros would never have left his inheritance to them" (ὡς δ' οὐδ' εἰ μηδέτερον τούτων ὑπῆρχε, μήτε ἔχθρα πρὸς τούτους μήτε φιλία πρὸς ἡμᾶς, οὐκ ἄν ποτε Ἀπολλόδωρος ἐπὶ τούτοις τὸν κλῆρον τοῦτον κατέλιπεν, οἶμαι καὶ ταῦθ' ὑμῖν ῥᾳδίως ἐπιδείξειν.) This is followed by an assertion that consideration for his οἶκος and tomb-cult was indeed Apollodoros' main reason for adopting a son. He had seen his intestate heirs neglecting the continuation of their deceased brother's οἶκος, and he was afraid that his own οἶκος would suffer the same fate, if he let his property pass to them. It would seem that the speaker expected his audience, that is the judges, to be more favourably disposed towards arguments concerning the tomb-cult and οἶκος of the deceased than if personal likes and dislikes were being offered as the main reason for adoption.

If it was in general more acceptable to the Athenians that a man would adopt out of consideration for his οἶκος and tomb-cult than because he disliked his intestate heirs, there is good reason to be sceptical when investigating the real link between adoption and the tomb-cult and οἶκος-

---

[42] Isaios VII.7.

concept in the IV. century on the basis of the representations in the forensic speeches. The latter may have been exaggerated considerably, while it may have been downright damaging to the cause of an adopted son, if he chose to represent his adoption as the result of a family-strife. If the assumption that adoption was the only means of disrupting the order of intestate succession is correct, we must reckon with the possibility that many adoptions were carried out with the main, or even sole aim of depriving disliked relatives of their share in the inheritance and/or conferring the inheritance on a favoured person who was not an intestate heir, whereas the wish to see his οἶκος continued may have played only a minor part in a IV. century-Athenian's decision to adopt an heir.

In the following paragraphs it will be investigated how the Athenians used adoption to disrupt the order of intestate succession. The main focus of the discussion will be on testamentary adoption. It is desirable to concentrate on this type of adoption in particular, since the γηροτροφία-aspect, as pointed out above, had probably only a minor impact, if any, on the decision to draw up a will, whereas it cannot be ruled out that adoption *inter vivos* functioned first and foremost as a means of securing support for the adopter in his old age. The working hypothesis of the following discussion is that when an Athenian decided to draw up a will, he was prompted either by consideration for the fate of his οἶκος and tomb-cult or his wish to disrupt the order of intestate succession, or a combination of both.

A certain type of will would appear to have been drawn up with the main purpose of ensuring the continuation of the οἶκος of the testator, namely those wills which provided for the adoption of an intestate heir. We know of two disputed adoptions of persons who both claimed to be the intestate heirs of their adoptive fathers. One is Pyrrhos' adoption of his sister's son, Endios (cat.no. 7), which is described in Isaios III, a speech delivered by Endios' natural brother. The other is the adoption of Chairestratos by his maternal uncle, Philoktemon (cat.no. 15). We are in no position to determine whether the two adoptees were in fact the intestate heirs of the adopters. In the case of Endios, we know that an alleged daughter of Pyrrhos had advanced a claim on Pyrrhos' inheritance after Endios' death, and she had barred the inheritance-suit instigated by Endios' natural brother by means of a διαμαρτυρία[43].

---

[43] Isaios III.2sq.

According to Chairestratos' opponents, Philoktemon had two paternal half-brothers[44] who would outrank his sister and her offspring in the order of intestate succession. Both Endios' brother and the speaker who delivered Isaios VI on behalf of Chairestratos as his συνήγορος allege that the children whose claims were advanced by their opponents were illegitimate and therefore not entitled to inherit[45]. But the problem of whether the speakers were speaking the truth or not need not concern us here. What matters in this context is that the speakers expected their audience to accept it as perfectly plausible that a childless man would choose an intestate heir as his adopted son.

In the next chapter it will be argued that a legitimate son of a woman who was her father's sole descendant was considered the intestate heir of his maternal grandfather, even if his mother had never been the object of an ἐπιδικασία. If that conclusion is accepted, then the four known instances of grandfathers who adopted the sons of their daughters *inter vivos* or by will must be counted among the known adoptions of intestate heirs[46]. Thus, they are a further indication that this kind of adoption was not alien to the Athenians. Hagnias' adoption of his niece may belong to this category as well; but the sources do not inform us of exactly how he was related to her. It is possible that she was the daughter of one of Hagnias' uterine half-siblings in which case she would rank very low in the order of intestate succession[47].

In any case, it is safe to assume that it did happen that a childless man chose an intestate heir as his adoptee. But how frequent was this kind of adoption? This is hard for us to tell, since adoptions of intestate heirs were probably the ones least likely to be disputed in the People's Court. Consider, for example, the case of Endios as represented by his brother in Isaios III. If Endios had not been adopted by Pyrrhos, he and his brother would have had to divide the inheritance of their father equally between themselves. Now, as a result of the adoption, Endios lost his

---

[44] Isaios VI.4, 12sq.
[45] E.g. Isaios III.3sqq., 13-18, Isaios VI.19-26.
[46] Cat.nos. 24, 28, 33, 35.
[47] See e.g. W.E. Thompson, *De Hagniae Hereditate*, pp.11sq. In fact, Theopompos who refers to this adoption in Isaios XI.8 states explicitly that she was not Hagnias' closest relative: "Now, when Hagnias was making his preparations before sailing out as an ambassador on this mission so beneficial to our city, he did not leave his property to us, his closest relatives, in case anything should happen to him; but adopted his niece as his daughter." ('Αγνίας οὖν, ὅτε ἐκπλεῖν παρεσκευάζετο πρεσβεύσων ἐπὶ ταύτας τὰς πράξεις αἳ τῇ πόλει συμφερόντως εἶχον, οὐκ ἐφ' ἡμῖν τοῖς ἐγγύτατα γένους, εἴ τι πάθοι, τὰ ὄντα κατέλιπεν, ἀλλ' ἐποιήσατο θυγατέρα αὑτοῦ ἀδελφιδῆν.)

right to inherit from his natural father which meant that his brother became the universal heir to his father's property. Thus, the adoption benefitted not only Endios, but his brother as well, so that the latter would have but little interest in objecting to the adoption being carried out.

On the other hand, there is no doubt that the Athenians often adopted persons who would not otherwise have been entitled to inherit. In nine out of the twelve wills recorded in the catalogue, the testators did disrupt the order of intestate succession. Admittedly, it is not safe to base any conclusions on these figures alone; the source material is much too biased to allow that. Of the nine wills which disrupted the order of intestate succession, seven were disputed in court, and disputed wills were probably more likely to be recorded in our sources than those that were accepted right away by the intestate heirs. In fact, five of the disputed wills are known to us from forensic speeches (Isaios I, IV, V, IX, and X) which had a direct bearing on the wills themselves. However, *Ath. Pol.* 35.2, that has been quoted in section 1 (and which will be quoted once more below) yields an additional piece of information that may be of interest to the present discussion.

The passage indicates that many testators chose beneficiaries who were *not* their intestate heirs. We are told that the Thirty Tyrants revised Solon's laws by deleting ambiguous provisions or provisions which were thought to give rise to excessive litigation, "for example by giving absolute authority to the law about bequeathing one's property to whomever one wants. They removed the troublesome addition 'if not affected by madness, senility, or persuaded by a woman', so that there would be no opportunity for sykophants." (...οἷον ‹τὸν› περὶ τοῦ δοῦναι τὰ ἑαυτοῦ ᾧ ἂν ἐθέλῃ κύριον ποιήσαντες καθάπαξ· τὰς δὲ προσούσας δυσκολίας, ' ἐὰν μὴ μανιῶν ἢ γήρων ἢ γυναικὶ πιθόμενος' ἀφεῖλον ὅπως μὴ ᾖ τοῖς συκοφάνταις ἔφοδος.) According to the author of *Ath. Pol.*, this revision was favourably received by the Athenians, as was the rest of the Thirty Tyrants' attempts to diminish the abuse of the Athenian law courts. From this it may perhaps be inferred that, although adoption of intestate heirs was practised by the Athenians, a great many testators took no heed of the claims of their intestate heirs; so many, in fact, that the disputed wills were a strain on the Athenian administration of justice. It must be borne in mind, however, that the *Ath. Pol.* is referring to the situation which arose in the aftermath of a great war and a period of famine where the number of inheritance-cases was probably larger than usual. On the other hand, the implication that wills were often disputed by the testator's intestate heir is corroborated e.g. by a remark made in Isaios III.61: "But all relatives by blood do not hesitate to advance their claims, bidding defiance to the adopted sons." (πρὸς δὲ τοὺς εἰσποιητοὺς ἅπαντες οἱ κατὰ γένος προσήκοντες ἀμφισβητεῖν ἀξιοῦσιν.) In his generalization, the speaker assumes that usually the beneficiaries in wills and the intestate heirs would not be identical. Thus, we must not see the nine disputed wills disrupting the order of intestate succession as exceptions to a rule that childless Athenians would normally adopt their intestate heirs.

It is widely held by modern scholars that wills were inextricably bound up with adoption in IV. century Athens. One of the most important assumptions on which this theory rests is that the Solonic law which conferred the right to 'dispose freely of one's property' on the childless Athenian was originally passed with the sole aim of allowing him to choose an heir for adoption *inter vivos*. According to this view, the Athenian will was but a variant of the original adoption *inter vivos*, a variant that had been developed secondarily after the law had been passed[48]. Thus, in IV. century Athens it was possible to adopt by will; but only in the Hellenistic age was the law interpreted as allowing the Athenians to bequeath their property in a will without adopting their beneficiaries. The IV. century is seen as a phase of transition in which the Athenian inheritance system was gradually secularized: adoption was still obligatory when choosing an heir in a will, but it was regarded as a mere formality which was at last abolished in the postclassical age. Although this view has been somewhat modified, it is nonetheless widely held that, in the IV. century, a childless Athenian could not appoint a universal heir in his will without adopting him (or her).

The questions of what Solon intended by passing his law, and how the phrase διατίθεσθαι τὰ ἑαυτοῦ was understood in the VI. century are bound up with the matter of property and ownership in this period. To enter this debate would be outside the scope of this work, and, in fact, the question is not all that relevant to the immediate issue. The main objective here is to determine how to interpret the sources bearing on

---

[48] Gernet (1955) is one of the most important contributions to the development of this theory. Gernet has been followed by e.g. Harrison (1968), but his arguments were countered by E.Ruschenbusch (1962). In more recent work such as MacDowell (1978) pp.99sq., Gernet's view has been modified considerably.

the working of the institution of adoption in the IV. century. Now, if the IV. century is seen as a phase of transition in which testamentary adoption was but a thin layer of varnish on top of an inheritance-system by then almost completely secularized, there is reason to be somewhat cautious when treating the tomb-cult and οἶκος motifs in the forensic speeches as a reflection of IV. century Athenian reality, even if it is safe to use them as sources for how adoption was ideologically construed in this period.

Evidence for the survival of adoption in Hellenistic and Roman Athens has been presented in an article recently published by the Copenhagen Epigraphy Group[49]. The fact that the Athenians still practised adoption after the close of the IV. century is an argument against seeing the IV. century as a phase of transition during which Athenian family-structure and ideas of the family underwent a radical change. In this chapter another discussion will be resumed, which will, hopefully, corroborate the assumption that, as regards the Athenian institution of adoption, the evidence points to continuity rather than change.

One of the arguments on which scholars have based their assumption that testamentary adoption ceased to be important in the course of the IV. century is that there is evidence for wills not providing for adoption in the Hellenistic era. Since it was impossible to draw up a will without adopting one's beneficiary in the IV. century, it may be inferred that the Athenian concept of "a will" had changed in the meantime. The question to be asked here is whether adoption *was* in fact obligatory when drawing up a will in the IV. century. If it was not; that is, if adoption depended on the wish of each individual testator to see his family-line continued and his tomb-cult taken care of, then each of the wills actually known to have provided for adoption will testify to the importance of private tomb-cult[50] and the οἶκος-concept as late as the IV. century. This will lend greater credibility to the rhetorical *topoi* referred to above. The question of whether there are any wills drawn up in the V. and IV. centuries which are known not have provided for adoption has been asked before[51], but it is hoped that the evidence for wills without

---

[49] L. Rubinstein *et al*. (1991).
[50] See S.C.Humphreys (1980b) for the view that Athenian *private* tomb cult grew in importance in the V. and IV. centuries.
[51] E.g. Lipsius (1905-15) pp.563sq., Bruck (1909), pp.96-141, Asheri (1963), Harrison (1968), pp.82sq. and pp.149sq., G.E.M. de Ste. Croix (1970), A.Biscardi, (1983), Mac Dowell (1978) p.101.

adoption to be discussed in the following paragraphs will allow the conclusion that adoption was *not* obligatory in the IV., or even V. centuries when choosing a testamentary heir.

A number of wills are known to have been drawn up by Athenians who left legitimate sons. Those of Konon, (Lysias XIX.39sqq.), Diodotos (Lysias XXXII.5sq.), Pasion (Dem. XXXVI, [Dem.] XLV, XLVI *pass.*), and Demosthenes the Elder all belong to this category. None of these provided for adoption, but, nevertheless, each is referred to as a διαθήκη, and the act of drawing up such a will is expressed by the verb διατίθεσθαι. Each of these wills contained provisions which reduced the shares of the testators' sons in the inheritance left by their fathers. The contents of Konon's will are especially striking: of his property worth ca. 40 mnas, only 17 were to pass to his son.

These examples have already been included in the discussion of the connection between wills and adoption. Scholars who are of the view that adoption was obligatory when drawing up a will reject them as evidence on the grounds that they were not in keeping with the provision in the Solonic law which restricted the right to διατίθεσθαι τὰ ἑαυτοῦ to Athenians without legitimate sons[52].

An argument to the contrary is the fact that three of these wills were considered legal. Neither Demosthenes the orator, nor the two sons of Diodotos ever challenged their father's wills; on the contrary, their guardians were prosecuted for having disregarded the obligations placed upon them by the terms of the wills[53]. Of course we may speculate on what would have been the outcome of a case, had the sons tried to challenge the validity of the wills in the People's Court, as Pasion's son, Apollodoros, did. But the fact that both Demosthenes the Orator and the speaker who attacks the guardian of Diodotos' sons in Lysias XXXII refer to the wills as evidence supporting their cases shows us that they expected their audience to react to the wills as valid documents. The speaker of Lysias XIX claims that Konon was εὖ φρονῶν when he drew up his will (41), and that the will must therefore be considered valid. There is no hint that Konon's son ever tried to challenge his father's will.

We have no evidence for the existence of a law permitting Athenians with legitimate male descendants to make wills. Apollodoros' attack on

---

[52] E.g. G.E.M. de Ste. Croix (1970), U.E.Paoli (1961).
[53] Dem.XXVII.13-16, XXVIII.6, 15sq.

his father's will in [Dem.] XLVI is an indication that such a law did not exist: his attack is primarily based on the provision in the Solonic law which restricted the right of διατίθεσθαι τὰ ἑαυτοῦ to men without legitimate sons. He would hardly have been able to get away with arguing on the basis of the Solonic law alone, if a law had existed which explicitly allowed certain testamentary dispositions to be valid even if the testator left legitimate sons[54]. It must be noted, however, that Apollodoros' interpretation of the law is generally rather heavy-handed. He claims, for example, that his father had not been in a position to make a will at all, because he had acquired rather than been born to Athenian citizenship: Pasion had been 'adopted' by the Athenian people (ἐπεποίητο ὑπὸ τοῦ δήμου πολίτης, 15), and since the law expressly forbade adopted sons to dispose of their property, Pasion's will should not be considered valid. On the other hand, Apollodoros is not the only one to claim that a will made by a man who had left legitimate sons was not to be valid; the same allegation is found in Isaios VI.28 and X.9.

A possible explanation of why it happened that three of the wills referred to above were accepted as valid after all may be that the law did not *unambiguously* restrict the right to draw up a will to those men who left no sons. The law only restricts to the childless men the right to dispose *freely* ("as one would like", ὅπως ἂν ἐθέλῃ) [55]. The law would thus allow the possible interpretation that a man was permitted to make certain testamentary dispositions which would be valid even if he left legitimate sons, provided that he had paid due heed to their claims. It is difficult, if not impossible, to tell what would have been considered 'due' by the Athenians in the IV. century. Apollodoros' argument in [Dem.] XLIV shows that a considerable range of interpretations of the law was possible in the IV. century, and as for the rights of a natural son, there is no hint that a legal definition existed in connection with the legislation on wills. Probably it was decided by the People's Court what was to be considered 'due' or 'acceptable' each time a natural son like Apollodoros tried to have his father's will invalidated.

It is important to point out that these wills are not distinguished by any difference in terminology from the wills drawn up by childless

---

[54] We know of a law (quoted in [Dem.] XLVI.24) that permitted Athenians with legitimate *minor* sons to draw up wills which would come into effect *only if* the sons died before coming of age. So this law does not allow for wills of the type described here.
[55] This is the conclusion drawn by A. Biscardi (1983), p.33.

men. Both types are referred to as διαθῆκαι, no matter whether the testator was childless or not. Thus, in the IV. century the Athenians did not distinguish terminologically between the wills which provided for adoption and those which did not: this will then mean that the verbs ποιεῖσθαι and διατίθεσθαι were not interchangeable[56].

In addition to the wills made by Athenians with legitimate sons, there are a number of examples of wills drawn up by childless men which nonetheless did not provide for adoption. Some of these have not, as far as I know, been adduced recently as evidence in the scholarly dispute referred to above.

1) In Lysias XIII.41 we are told that Dionysodoros "made dispositions regarding his private affairs as he saw fit" (τά τε οἰκεῖα διέθετο ὅπως αὐτῷ ἐδόκει) after his imprisonment by the Thirty Tyrants. It is important to note that the expression used here is very close to the wording of the Solonic law-text. Dionysodoros was childless when he made these dispositions, but his wife was pregnant which would undoubtedly have influenced them. Unfortunately, the text does not provide any information regarding the contents of his (perhaps oral) will or how, and to what extent, he paid heed to the claims of a potential male heir.

2) Polyeuktos left two daughters and a will (Dem. XLI.10), and in this case, too, the expression διέθετο is used. The speaker does not refer to the exact contents of the will, but it appears from the circumstances of the lawsuit in which Dem. XLI was delivered that the will did not provide for adoption. The lawsuit was initiated when Polyeuktos' two daughters were to divide his property between them after his death. There is no indication that Polyeuktos had intended to adopt either of his sons-in-law, and no mention of any third person who was to be adopted.

3) In Isaios VII.6 there is another instance of a will not providing for adoption. Allegedly, Eupolis had claimed that his childless brother, Mneson, had left him his entire property (φάσκων αὐτῷ δοῦναι τὸν ἀδελφόν)[57].

4) Alkibiades' brother-in-law, Kallias, was afraid that Alkibiades would try to murder him in order to possess his property. For this

---

[56] As claimed by e.g. Gernet (1955), p.122, but see Ruschenbusch (1962), pp.308sq.
[57] This was actually accepted as a possible will without adoption by Bruck (1909), p.151 who sees it as an exceptional case "im Wiederspruch zu dem Grundgedanken des attischen Erbrechts", along with Plato's will (ex. 5).

reason he bequeathed it to the Athenian people "in case he would die childless" (εἴ πως τελευτήσειεν ἄπαις)[58]. The expression διαθήκη is not employed here, nor is the verb διατίθεσθαι. Instead, as in the preceding example, ἔδωκε is used to denote Kallias' action. But this is no reason for doubting that the meaning is that Eupolis and Kallias did leave wills. δοῦναι is regularly used in contemporary paraphrases of the Solonic law-text itself, instead of διατίθεσθαι[59]. That Kallias did not intend to adopt the entire Athenian people is obvious.

5) Plato's will is recorded in Diogenes Laertios 3.41-43. In his will, he made one of his relatives his universal heir. Although scholars usually assume that Plato adopted his heir, the will itself contains no provision to this effect.

These five examples[60] show that it was indeed possible to make a will without adopting the beneficiary in the IV. century, and perhaps even earlier, as 1) above. This means that each of the testamentary *adoptions* recorded in our sources may be interpreted as an indicator of the importance, to each individual testator, of the continuation of his family-line and his tomb-cult[61]. If a testator's sole aim was to ensure the disruption of the order of intestate succession, he would be able to achieve this without necessarily having to adopt an heir.

---

[58] [And.] IV.15 and Plut. *Alcibiades*, 8.4. I only adduce this example with a certain hesitation, since [And.] IV is spurious and may well be a Hellenistic rhetorical exercise. The relationship between [And.] IV.15 and Plut. *Alcibiades*, 8.4 is hard to establish. The wording of the two passages differs as does the order of presentation of Alkibiades' familyscandals. The two accounts furnish slightly different details, so if Plutarch used [And.] IV as a source for Alkibiades' private life, it was certainly not his only one. On the other hand, if [And.] IV is to be identified as a political pamphlet of the late IV. century, as done by Dover (1974), p.8, n.1, it is still relevant as a source for the Athenian IV. century practice of bequest. The will has been discussed by Bruck (1909) pp.83sqq., who accepts it (with reservations) as a "Schenkung auf den Todesfall". However, Bruck's suggestion that there was a legal distinction in Athens between a "Schenkung auf den Todesfall" (which was a contract) and a "Testament" (which was a unilateral act) is hard to accept on the basis of the available evidence, and this part of his hypothesis has hardly left any trace in the subsequent debate. Even Bruck himself faces the difficulty that "ein terminologischer Unterschied zwischen Schenkung, Schenkung von Todeswegen und Legat ist jedenfalls nirgends erkennbar".

[59] Dem.XX.102, Isaios IX.13, *Ath.Pol.* 35.2.

[60] A sixth example is perhaps the one found in Dio.Hal. *De Isaeo*, 15, where Dionysios paraphrases Isaios' speech πρὸς Ἀριστογείτονα καὶ Ἄρχιππον, "ἐν ᾗ κλήρου τις ἀμφισβητῶν, ἀδελφὸς ὢν τοῦ τελευτήσαντος, προκαλεῖται τὸν ἔχοντα τάφανῆ χρήματα εἰς ἐμφανῶν κατάστασιν, ὁ δὲ τοῦ κλήρου κρατῶν παραγράφεται τὴν κλῆσιν, δεδόσθαι λέγων ἑαυτῷ τὰ χρήματα κατὰ διαθήκας", but the paraphrase is much too superficial to allow any safe conclusions.

[61] In fact, only seven of the twelve wills recorded in the catalogue can be said with certainty to have provided for adoption. In those cases where it is doubtful whether the will in question provided for the adoption of the beneficiary, the will has been marked with an (*) in the catalogue.

Chapter 5: Adoption and ἐπίκληροι

It is beyond doubt that there was a close connection between the institution of adoption and another important aspect of Athenian inheritance law, the institution of ἐπίκληροι, "heiresses". If a man left only female descendants, his daughter or daughters would become ἐπίκληροι at his death. Women had no right of inheritance in our sense of the word: they could not dispose legally of property worth more than one medimnos of barley, and they were thus not allowed to dispose of the inheritance themselves. Therefore, special rules applied to a woman who had no brother of the same father at her father's death.

An ἐπίκληρος was inextricably tied to the inheritance left by her father. At his death she would be the object of an ἐπιδικασία along with the inheritance. The nearest male relative of her father (that is, the one who would otherwise have been entitled to inherit according to the order of intestate succession, if the deceased had left no daughters) would only get control over the inheritance, if he consented to marry her. Even then he was not considered the actual *heir*, since, ultimately, the right to the inheritance devolved on the children he would produce in his marriage to the ἐπίκληρος. According to the law, he would just be administering the property until his son or sons came of age.

In 14 of the 33 adoptions recorded in the catalogue we find that women were involved. Three of these (cat. nos.9, 13, 17) were adopted daughters who were probably to be treated as ἐπίκληροι of their adoptive fathers (we do not know what actually happened to them), while 11 of the women concerned were claimed or claiming to be the sole legitimate, natural descendants of their fathers. These 11 women will be the main concern of this chapter.

Three daughters whose rights had allegedly been violated as a result of an adoption are 1) Pyrrhos' daughter Phile (see cat.no.7), 2) the daughters of Diokles' stepfather (see cat.no.19), and 3) the daughter of Aristarchos (see cat.no.10).

4) One daughter was married to her adoptive brother, namely Polyeuktos' daughter, Kleiokrateia (see cat.no.2).

5) The daughter of Euboulides II had been treated as an ἐπίκληρος, and one of her sons was subsequently adopted into her father's οἶκος (see cat.no.24).

Furthermore, we find five examples of grandsons who had been adopted by their maternal grandfathers, probably *inter vivos* or by will. We may safely infer from the fact that their grandfathers adopted them that the former left daughters, but no legitimate natural sons. These adopted sons are 6) Diokles, the son of Themistokles (cat.no. 28), 7) Kyronides (cat.no. 30), 8) Phainippos (cat.no. 35), 9) Archimachos (cat.no. 33), and 10) Lykophron (cat.no. 36).

The last case, 11), is the complicated one described in Isaios VI (cat.no.15). The mother of Chairestratos and her sister were, according to the speaker of Isaios VI, the only surviving legitimate children of Euktemon. But one of Euktemon's sons had, before his death, made a will in which he named Chairestratos as his adopted son. The other sister had no male offspring, and the speaker claims that she ought to be considered an ἐπίκληρος, even though the speaker himself alleges that Chairestratos was to be considered the lawful son of Euktemon's son according to the latter's will. Of these 11 adoptions involving natural daughters, 1)-3) were allegedly illegal, 4)-10) were represented as legal, and 11) seems to me to be impossible to determine.

These cases will form the basis of the following investigation of how adoption functioned both as a supplement and as an alternative to the institution of ἐπίκληροι.

1. Adoption as a supplement to the ἐπίκληρος-institution

Modern scholars often debate the purpose or purposes of the ἐπίκληρος-institution in IV. century Athens. The traditional view is that the main aim of the legislation was to ensure the continuation of family-lines through daughters in those cases where their fathers had left no male offspring to succeed them. But this view has been challenged recently[1], and with good reason. For although the legislation concerning ἐπίκληροι aimed at making sure that the inheritance would pass to male descendants of the deceased *via* the ἐπίκληρος, these rules were in

---

[1] Schaps (1979) pp.39-42.

themselves no guarantee that his family-line would be continued. The sons of an ἐπίκληρος would belong to their father's οἶκος, in spite of the fact that they were also considered the heirs of their maternal grandfather. The only means of preventing the latter's οἶκος from dying out would have been posthumous adoption: a son born from the ἐπίκληρος could be made the adopted son of his grandfather, whereby the continued existence of his grandfather's οἶκος would be ensured for at least another generation.

We know only one certain example of such an adoption, namely the posthumous adoption of Euboulides III into his maternal grandfather's οἶκος, which is described in [Dem.] XLIII and has been treated in greater detail in chapter 3. But the fact that we know of only one posthumous adoption of this kind need not mean that such adoptions were only exceptionally carried out; it may rather reflect the fact that these adoptions would only rarely, or hardly ever, be disputed. The only person who would stand to gain from having the adoption overruled by the People's Court would be the natural brother (or brothers) of the adoptee, since it was only the sons of an ἐπίκληρος who had a claim on the property left by her father. A brother of the adoptee, on the other hand, would probably often consider the adoption an advantage to himself. The adoptee lost his right to inherit from his natural father as a result of the adoption, and his share would thus devolve on his natural brother. The fewer brothers an Athenian had, the larger his own share in his father's inheritance. This means that it is hard for us to determine how often adoption was used as a supplement to the ἐπίκληρος-institution, since undisputed posthumous adoptions are less likely to have been recorded in the sort of sources we have for the institution in the IV. century.

The three recorded adoptions of women may be an indication that this kind of posthumous adoption was not uncommon. A testator would not ensure the continuation of his family-line by choosing a female adoptee: she would have the status of an ἐπίκληρος at his death, and her children would belong to the οἶκος of her prospective husband. From this point of view, adopting a woman would only make sense, if the adopter could have some confidence that a son born from his adopted daughter would later be transferred to his οἶκος by means of adoption. He may have stipulated in his will that a posthumous adoption was later to be carried out: Hagnias' will, for example, may have included such a stipulation, in addition to the provision that his uterine half-brother was to be his heir, if his adopted daughter died childless. But if a testator had not taken care to add such a stipulation, how safely could he rely on his heirs carrying out a posthumous adoption on their own initiative? Was the κύριος, that is, the husband of the ἐπίκληρος *obliged* in any way to provide for a posthumous adoption of one of the sons born to him from the ἐπίκληρος?

We may be able to answer this question by turning to the law quoted in [Dem.] XLVI.20: "and when someone is born from an ἐπίκληρος, and when he is two years past entering puberty[2], he shall be in control of the property and provide his mother with an allowance of food". (καὶ ἐὰν ἐξ ἐπικλήρου τις γένηται, καὶ ἅμα ἡβήσῃ ἐπὶ διετές, κρατεῖν τῶν χρημάτων, τὸν δὲ σῖτον μετρεῖν τῇ μητρί.) This law establishes that the son of an ἐπίκληρος is to be considered the rightful heir to his maternal grandfather's property, and stipulates the age he must have reached before assuming control. It also states that he is to be responsible for supporting the ἐπίκληρος, his mother, materially. Adoption is not mentioned as a requirement that must be met, before the heir could enter into possession. In fact, the law does not mention any obligations incumbent on the heir as regards the οἶκος of his maternal grandfather. The reason why adoption is left out of this law may of course be that it was taken for granted that the heir would be posthumously adopted, or the requirement may have been stated in another law lost to us. But other passages from the orators in which this law is referred to point to the conclusion that, in the IV. century, posthumous adoption was *not* a legal requirement[3]. In all these passages it is the children, οἱ παῖδες, of the ἐπίκληρος who are referred to as the rightful heirs of the ἐπίκληρος' father. The repeated use of the plural in this context is a clear indication that the right to the inheritance was not reserved for a single son of the ἐπίκληρος, who could only take possession of the inheritance after having

---

[2] The wording ἐπὶ διετὲς ἡβῆσαι has been discussed by Labarbe (1956), where he argues that the κούρειον was a rite de passage, marking the threshold of manhood, which took place at the age of 16. According to his view, then, ἐπὶ διετὲς ἡβῆσαι means to reach the age of 18 (16+2), corresponding to the age of civic majority. Golden (1990) holds that in pre-Cleisthenic Athens, legal maturity of a boy was marked by the offering of the κούρειον in the boy's phratry, and that this offering would take place two years after the onset of puberty (14+2). But after the Cleisthenic reforms, the Athenians used the phrase to denote civic majority (18), "even though its literal meaning no longer corresponded to the age of those it described" (p.27).
[3] Isaios III.50, VIII.31, X.12, πρὸς Λυκίβιον περὶ ἐπικλήρου (frg. XXIV, Baiter & Sauppe), [Dem.] XLVI.20, Hypereides frg.LXIII (ed. Chr. Jensen, Bibl. Teubneriana, 1917).

been posthumously adopted. *All* her (male) children were considered the heirs to her father's property. This shows that inheriting from one's maternal grandfather was not conditional on having been posthumously adopted.

That posthumous adoption was by no means obligatory may be further corroborated by a passage from Isaios III. This speech was delivered in a lawsuit concerning the inheritance left by Pyrrhos. Pyrrhos had adopted one of his sister's two sons, Endios, in a will, but Endios died childless 23 years later[4], which meant that the property had once more to be the object of an ἐπιδικασία. Endios' brother advanced a claim on behalf of his mother, but this claim was barred with a διαμαρτυρία made by the husband of Phile who claimed that she was the lawful daughter of Pyrrhos.[5] The only way in which Endios' brother could proceed from there was to instigate a δίκη ψευδομαρτυρίων against Phile's husband, claiming that Phile was an illegitimate child. Having won this suit he prosecuted another witness who had supported Phile's husband, namely Nikodemos, the brother of Phile's mother. It was in this lawsuit that Isaios III was delivered. In (72-73) the speaker tries to prove from Pyrrhos' behaviour that Pyrrhos himself had not recognised Phile as his daughter. He claims that the adoption of Endios would have been completely superfluous, if Phile had been the legitimate daughter of Pyrrhos, since Pyrrhos "could have introduced his daughter born to him from Nikodemos' sister to his phratry as his legitimate child leaving her as ἐπίκληρος with all his property, and he could have stipulated that one of the sons born from his daughter be introduced as his (posthumously adopted) son". (ἐξὸν...τὴν θυγατέρα τὴν ἐκ ταύτης ἀποφανθεῖσαν εἶναι εἰς τοὺς φράτερας εἰσαγαγόντι ὡς οὖσαν γνησίαν ἑαυτῷ, ἐπὶ ἅπαντι τῷ κλήρῳ ἐπίδικον καταλιπεῖν αὐτήν, καὶ ἐπισκῆψαι τῶν γιγνομένων <ἐκ> τῆς θυγατρὸς παίδων εἰσαγαγεῖν υἱὸν ἑαυτῷ.) The fact that Pyrrhos would have had to issue a stipulation that the adoption take place may be read as an indication that adoption was not *legally* an obligatory supplement to the ἐπίκληρος-institution. In section three of this chapter it will be demonstrated that grandsons would sometimes be adopted by the maternal grandfathers by means of testamentary adoptions or adoptions *inter vivos*, another indication that a father with

---

[4] Isaios III.1.
[5] Isaios III.3.

an only daughter could not safely rely on his daughter's κύριος to provide for a posthumous adoption.

The provisional conclusion of this section is that we have no means of telling how frequently adoption was used as a supplement to the ἐπίκληρος-institution. It certainly did not work automatically: the continuation of the οἶκος of the ἐπίκληρος' father must have depended on the willingness of her husband to ensure that an adoption took place. On the other hand, it cannot be ruled out that the heirs were under a strong moral obligation to carry out a posthumous adoption. Social pressure may be just as important and, indeed, effective as formal legal requirements, but as will be shown in section 3 of this chapter, the precautions made by Athenians who left daughters but no sons to ensure that their family-lines be continued indicate that the moral obligations were not so strong as to guarantee that posthumous adoption would be carried out by the heirs.

2. Adoption as an alternative to the ἐπίκληρος-institution

Isaios III which has been referred to above may prove a convenient starting-point for this section. In (73) Endios' brother argues in the following way: what reasons could Pyrrhos possibly have had for adopting Endios, if he already had a legitimate daughter? "Was it that he had other relatives who were more closely related to him than we were, and that he adopted my brother because he wanted to prevent them from claiming his daughter in an ἐπιδικασία?" (πότερον ὅτι προσήκοντες αὐτῷ ἐγγυτέρω γένους ἡμῶν ἦσαν ἄλλοι, οὓς βουλόμενος τὴν ἐπιδικασίαν τῆς θυγατρὸς ἀποστερῆσαι ἐποιεῖτο τὸν ἀδελφὸν υἱὸν αὐτῷ;). Endios' brother then goes on to show that Pyrrhos had in fact adopted an heir who would have had the best claim to his daughter's hand anyway; for this reason, he argues, the adoption would have been pointless, if Phile had really been Pyrrhos' legitimate daughter.

In chapter 4 it has been shown how the wish to disrupt the order of intestate succession, combined with the wish to ensure the continuation of οἶκος and tomb-cult, could prompt a childless Athenian to adopt an heir. This last aspect is deliberately suppressed by Endios' brother, who wants to prove that Phile was illegitimate by referring to her father's will. He has already mentioned posthumous adoption of one of Phile's future sons as a way in which Pyrrhos could have ensured the continuation of his line, if Phile had really been legitimate. But in order to prove that Pyrrhos' testamentary adoption of Endios was incompatible with Phile's being his legitimate daughter, the speaker has to counter another possible argument from his opponents: an Athenian who left an only daughter might have had even stronger reasons for adopting a son. For in this way he could prevent his daughter from being awarded to his nearest male relative as an ἐπίκληρος.

In addition to the concerns which might make a childless Athenian decide to adopt an heir (γηροτροφία, tomb-cult, continuation of his οἶκος, and hostility to his intestate heirs) the father of an only daughter may have had his daughter's best interests at heart. If he left a considerable inheritance to go along with her, it would be highly likely that his nearest male relative would claim her, regardless of his own age and marital status. By adopting a husband for her *inter vivos* or by will he might be able to prevent this from happening and instead ensure that she would get married to a husband of his own choice. That such considerations did actually operate from time to time may be inferred from the plot of Menander's *Aspis*, although the comedy is of a later date than the period with which we are concerned here. In *Aspis*, the main intrigue is centred on an attempt made by benevolent characters in the play to prevent the greedy old Smikrines from claiming his niece in marriage as an ἐπίκληρος. Their reason for trying to doublecross Smikrines is apparently that he is too old to make a suitable husband for the young heroine[6]. Of course we cannot rule out the possibility that the Athenian outlook on family-life had changed so drastically during the IV. century that Menander's comedies cannot be used to supplement the evidence found in the corpus of Athenian forensic oratory. It has been claimed that the conflicts between legal regulations on the one hand and the individual characters and their emotions on the other in Menander's comedies herald a change in the Athenian concept of the family which was to come into full effect in the Hellenistic period[7]. But an argument against this assumption is the fact that we do find the same conflict expressed in the orators if only in slightly different and more moderate

---

[6] *Aspis*, 258-269.
[7] See e.g. Mossé (1989a) and MacDowell (1982).

terms; and the difference in expression may be due only to the fact that we are dealing with two different genres.

But it was not only those fathers whose daughters were still unmarried who might resort to adopting a son as a way of preventing their daughters from becoming ἐπίκληροι In Isaios III.64 the speaker hints at the problems that may arise if a brotherless woman had already been given away in marriage before her father died. At his death she would still be an ἐπίκληρος, and if we are to believe the speaker of Isaios III, this could lead to her marriage being dissolved, if her father's relatives wanted to claim her in marriage: "those married women who have been given in marriage by their fathers - and who could possibly be better at making decisions regarding a woman's marriage than her father? - the law commands that even women who have been married in this way may be claimed in an ἐπιδικασία by their closest relatives, if their father dies without leaving them any legitimate brothers, and up to the present time many married men have had their wives taken away from them." (τὰς μὲν ὑπὸ τῶν πατέρων ἐκδοθείσας καὶ συνοικούσας ἀνδράσι γυναῖκας - περὶ ὧν τίς ἂν ἄμεινον ἢ ὁ πατὴρ βουλεύσαιτο; - καὶ τὰς οὕτω δοθείσας, ἂν ὁ πατὴρ αὐτῶν τελευτήσῃ μὴ καταλιπὼν αὐταῖς γνησίους ἀδελφούς, τοῖς ἐγγύτατα γένους ἐπιδίκους ὁ νόμος εἶναι κελεύει, καὶ πολλοὶ συνοικοῦντες ἤδη ἀφῄρηνται τὰς ἑαυτῶν γυναῖκας). Here we find the speaker contrasting the rigidity of the legislation on ἐπίκληροι to the individual father and his capacity to arrange the most suitable marriage for his daughter. And we find an even stronger opposition between "law" and "the individual" in Isaios X.19, which is quoted fully below in section 3 of this chapter. Here the speaker claims that his father allowed the relatives of the speaker's mother to cheat her out of her inheritance, because he was afraid to lose her. Her relatives had threatened to have the marriage dissolved, if the speaker's father persisted in advancing her claim as her κύριος. Apparently, the speaker expects his audience to accept his father's devotion to his wife as a valid excuse for his failing to recover the inheritance, which she was allegedly entitled to possess according to the law. Admittedly, there is a considerable difference between, on the one hand, the speaker of Isaios III, who refers to the law as a matter of fact, and the sentiments expressed by the characters in Menander's *Aspis* on the other, but this does not prove that the Athenian concept of the family had changed during the IV. century. It may simply be due to the fact that the rhetoric of the stage of the Athenian lawcourts differed from the rhetoric of the comical stage, as pointed out in chapter 1.

Section 3) will discuss how adoption of daughters' sons was used as a means of safeguarding a marriage arranged by the father of a prospective ἐπίκληρος against claims advanced by his relatives after his death. Adopting his daughter's husband was another way of doing this, but it is impossible to tell how often adoption was actually employed in connection with only daughters. It has been claimed that, in the IV. century, adoption of the husband of the prospective ἐπίκληρος was a widely used alternative to the ἐπίκληρος-institution.[8], but the truth is that there is no evidence to corroborate this assumption. We know of only one instance where adoption was used in this way: in Dem.XLI.3-5 we are told that Polyeuktos adopted his brother-in-law, Leokrates, to whom he gave his youngest daughter, Kleiokrateia[9] in marriage. The marriage was later dissolved, and the adoption was cancelled. Unfortunately, the text does not state whether the cancellation of the adoption was an automatic consequence of the divorce, or whether a separate procedure was required. The speaker seems to assume that his audience would expect the divorce to entail annulment of the adoption.

This leads to the question of whether a father could adopt a son without stipulating that the adoptee was to marry his daughter. It is generally assumed by modern scholars that in such a case adoption was conditional on marriage. This assumption is partly based on the following passage from Isaios III.68 which is usually interpreted to the effect that, if the adopter had a daughter, the adopted son would be required to marry her[10]. "For the law states explicitly that it is permitted to dispose of one's property in whatever way one would like, provided that one does not leave male legitimate children. If one leaves female children, [the dispositions have to be] with them". (ὁ γὰρ νόμος διαρρήδην λέγει ἐξεῖναι διαθέσθαι ὅπως ἂν ἐθέλῃ τις τὰ ἑαυτοῦ, ἐὰν μὴ παῖδας γνησίους καταλίπῃ ἄρρενας. ἂν δὲ θηλείας καταλίπῃ, σὺν ταύταις.)

No doubt, this was a possible interpretation of the law in the IV. century, too (this is the one propounded e.g. by the speaker of Isaios III[11]). But our problem is that we simply do not have enough examples

---

[8] See e.g. MacDowell (1978) p.95, R.Sealey, (1990) p.30.
[9] *Hesperia* VI (1937) p.341, see cat.no. 2.
[10] Gernet (1955) p.136, Harrison (1968) p.85 and 151, Schaps (1979), p.32 , Just (1989), p.95.
[11] See esp. 41sqq., and cf. Isaios X.13.

to show what would be the "normal" way of combining adoption with the concern for the adopter's daughters. The case of Leokrates is complicated by the fact that Polyeuktos did in fact have two daughters. The eldest was married to the speaker of Dem. XLI by ἐγγύη with a dowry. Her husband was not adopted by Polyeuktos; even so the arrangement appears to have been acceptable to the parties concerned.

A parallel to the situation of Polyeuktos' elder daughter is found in Menander's *Dyskolos*, where Knemon adopts his stepson Gorgias while his daughter is married off with half of her father's property as her dowry[12]. This may reflect another possible interpretation of the letter of the law: if the testator/adopter leaves daughters he must *include* them in his dispositions (διαθέσθαι σὺν ταύταις), that is, pay due heed to their claims (and ultimately the claims of their descendants). And we must assume that it would be left to the People's Court to decide, in each individual case of doubt, what could be accepted as "due"[13]. Even if the adopter chose an arrangement resembling that of Knemon, the adoption would in any case prevent his daughter from becoming ἐπίδικος, provided that the adoption had taken place *inter vivos* [14]. In that case the adoptee was allowed to succeed to the adopter's property without prior ἐπιδικασία which meant that neither the property of his adoptive father, nor the latter's daughters were legally ἐπίδικοι.

So, adoption could operate as an alternative to the ἐπίκληρος-institution in three different ways: a father could safeguard an already existing marriage by adopting his daughter's husband *inter vivos* or by will, or he could adopt a prospective husband for her (e.g. in case he died while she was still too young to marry), or, thirdly, he could prevent her

---

[12] v.738.
[13] I doubt whether we can draw any safe conclusions as regards the rights of only daughters of the kind that e.g. MacDowell has suggested on the basis of evidence from Menander's comedies (1978 and 1982).
[14] Paoli (1961) classifies the adoption of Gorgias as a *testamentary* adoption. And, in fact, we do not hear anything about Gorgias' being introduced to Knemon's phratry or deme. On the other hand, we must be very careful not to push the evidence of Menander's comedies too far. The fact that Knemon makes his dispositions without calling witnesses or following the normal procedure, and the fact that his stepson replies "OK! I accept all this!" (ἀλλὰ δέχομαι ταῦτα πάντα, v.748) may simply be due to dramatic economy: it is Knemon's very decision to adopt as a result of his accident which is the focus of attention in this scene, not necessarily the way he goes about it. At the same time we must remember that Knemon as a character is antisocial, his behaviour in shunning society in general is represented as abnormal, and it is possible to interpret the fact that he regards the adoption as valid without having obtained the accept of society as adding to Menander's picture of the eccentric loner.

from becoming ἐπίδικος simply by adopting a son *inter vivos*, no matter whether the adoptee was to marry her or not.

Finally, it must be noted that the Athenians apparently also used wills not providing for adoption to nominate husbands for their only daughters. In Isaios VII.9 there is a reference to a will in which a husband was nominated for the testator's adopted daughter without being adopted himself. This is, unfortunately, the only known example of such a will (although Lysias frg. XXXI may be related to a similar case), and the will never came into operation, as the testator later decided to adopt a son *inter vivos*. We have thus no means of telling how his collaterals would have reacted to his will, and whether it would be possible for them, having accepted her status as an ἐπίκληρος by virtue of the will, to persuade the judges that they still had a claim on her hand. However, it would seem that such wills nominating a husband for a prospective ἐπίκληρος without adopting him were not uncommon. In his *Wasps*, lines 583-586, Aristophanes plays upon the judges' reaction to those wills drawn up by fathers wanting to nominate husbands of their own choice for their only daughters[15]. There is no hint in this passage that adoption was in any way involved. Since the conclusion of the previous chapter was that it was indeed possible for a IV. century Athenian to bequeath his property without necessarily adopting his beneficiary, we must assume that it would also be possible to nominate a husband for one's daughter in a will without adopting him. Therefore, whenever we do come across an Athenian who chose to adopt his son-in-law, the actual adoption testifies to that Athenian's concern for the continuation of his οἶκος, however numerous the other factors which also prompted his decision.

3. Adoption of daughters' sons

In addition to adoption of a husband for the ἐπίκληρος which has been described in section 2), there was another type of adoption which may also have served as an alternative to the ἐπίκληρος-institution. In our

---

[15] κἄν ἀποθνῄσκων ὁ πατὴρ τῳ δῷ καταλείπων παῖδ' ἐπίκληρον,
κλάειν ἡμεῖς μακρὰ τὴν κεφαλὴν εἰπόντες τῇ διαθήκῃ
καὶ τῇ κόγχῃ τῇ πάνυ σεμνῶς τοῖς σημείοισιν ἐπούσῃ,
ἔδομεν ταύτην ὅστις ἂν ἡμᾶς ἀντιβολήσας ἀναπείσῃ.

sources five instances are recorded of daughters' sons having been adopted by their grandfathers (cat. nos.28, 30, 33, 35, 36). In the catalogue these adoptions have been registered as adoptions of type unknown, but in four cases (cat. nos. 28, 33, 35, 36), the wording of the passages that refer to the adoptions seems to suggest that the adoptive fathers had played an active part in the procedure. The verb ποιέω is used in the middle voice with the adopters as subject which makes it relatively safe to rule out posthumous adoption as a possibility[16]. It may be assumed, then, that the adoptions were carried out by the grandfathers themselves, either by will or *inter vivos*, and these adoptions may be seen as another way in which an Athenian could prevent his only daughter from becoming ἐπίδικος at his death.

The adoptions belonging to this category may be seen in the light of a complication inherent in the Athenian ἐπίκληρος-institution which has already been touched on in the previous section of this chapter. It sometimes happened that a brotherless woman was given in marriage by her father to a man who was not her father's nearest relative. There may have been various reasons why such a situation would arise, the most important being that an Athenian woman was considered marriageable already at the age of 14 or 15. In some cases, presumably, her father would not yet have abandoned hope that he would eventually produce a son, and he may not have wanted to leave her unmarried until the matter had been clarified. Another possible situation can be imagined: the woman actually had a brother at the time when she had reached the age of marriage, but if her brother died childless while their father was still alive she would be considered an ἐπίκληρος when her father died. This situation was bound to cause problems, as has already been illustrated with the passage from Isaios III.64 which has been quoted above. The speaker of Isaios III claims that the relatives of an ἐπίκληρος who had been given in marriage by her father could demand that her marriage be dissolved, so that she could be made the object of an ἐπιδικασία.

---

[16] [Dem.] XLII.21, [Dem.] XLIII.37, Plut. *Mor.* 843A, *Them.*32. To denote the adopter's active act of adoption, the middle voice of the verb ποιέω is always used ([Dem.] XLIV.25, 34, 46, 51, 61, 63, 64, 65, Isaios II.1, 2, 11-14, 16, 17, 19, 20, 22, 23, 28, 37, 41, 45, 46, III.1, 41, 75, 76, IV.19, VI.3, 5, 6, 7, 9, 51, 53, 63, VII.1, 2, 3, 4, 28, 30, 33, VIII.36, IX.1, 7, 16, 21, 31, 33, 34, 36, XI.8, 9, 41, 45) while the active voice is used to denote the act of carrying out a posthumous adoption on behalf of somebody else (Isaios VII.31,44, VIII.40, X.11, 12, 14, 16, 17, XI.49, [Dem.] XLIII.15, 78, [Dem.] XLIV.19, 24, 27, 41, 43, 55, 63).

His allegation may be further corroborated by the argument found in Isaios X.19. The speaker of Isaios X is advancing a claim on the inheritance left by his maternal grandfather. His mother had never been made the object of an ἐπιδικασία: according to the speaker her relatives had possessed themselves of her father's inheritance and had married her off to a man outside the ἀγχιστεία, in spite of the fact that she ought to have been considered an ἐπίκληρος and treated as such[17]. The speaker then goes on to explain why his father had never demanded, on behalf of his wife, that her relatives restore her father's property to her. "My father was married to my mother having accepted her formally as his wife with a dowry, and he did not have the means of recovering the inheritance which my opponents here were exploiting. When he, at my mother's request, talked to them about it, they threatened him that they would claim her hand in an ἐπιδικασία and obtain it, if he did not consent to have her with a dowry only. My father would have let them enjoy the property even if it had been twice as big in order to avoid losing my mother." (ὁ γὰρ πατὴρ οὑμὸς ἐπὶ προικὶ ἐγγυησάμενος τὴν ἐμὴν μητέρα συνῴκει, τὸν δὲ κλῆρον τούτων καρπουμένων οὐκ εἶχεν ὅπως εἰσπράξαιτο· ὅτε γὰρ περὶ αὐτοῦ λόγους ἐποιήσατο τῆς μητρὸς κελευούσης, οὗτοι ταῦτα αὐτῷ ἠπείλησαν, αὐτοὶ ἐπιδικασάμενοι αὐτὴν ἕξειν, εἰ μὴ βούλοιτο αὐτὸς ἐπὶ προικὶ ἔχειν. ὁ δὲ πατήρ, ὥστε τῆς μητρὸς μὴ στερηθῆναι, καὶ δὶς τοσαῦτα χρήματα εἴασεν ἂν αὐτοὺς καρποῦσθαι.)

A father who wished to safeguard the marriage of his only daughter against the prospective claims advanced by his relatives had the option of adopting her husband as his son, as shown in the previous section, but there was also another way of achieving this: he could adopt a child already born to his daughter and her husband. This would have had the same effect as an adoption of the daughter's husband. The grandson would be regarded legally as his mother's brother as a consequence of the adoption, and thus his mother would not be considered ἐπίδικος at her father's death.

It may be asked whether such an adoption would have been at all necessary to achieve this aim. Many scholars hold that once a son had been produced in the marriage of a prospective ἐπίκληρος and her husband by ἐγγύη, her relatives could no longer claim her hand in marriage. But there is not total agreement on this issue, and no

---

[17] Isaios X.5sq.

conclusive proof has ever been adduced[18]. The question is bound up with that of the rights of a grandson to the inheritance left by his maternal grandfather, if he had been born in a marriage contracted not by ἐπιδικασία, but by ἐγγύη. Did he have the right of a male descendant, that is the right to enter (ἐμβατεύειν) without prior ἐπιδικασία? And could he bar ἐπιδικασίαι instigated by male relatives of his mother who wanted to claim his mother in marriage as an ἐπίκληρος? If not, we may want to know how it would affect the rights of this grandson, if his mother was claimed as an ἐπίκληρος. He may have been considered on a par with his prospective half-brothers born in his mother's marriage to the successful claimant. But it is also conceivable that he would be entitled only to his mother's dowry which she brought into her first marriage[19].

If we try to answer these questions by looking at the actual cases presented in the law-court speeches, the answer seems to be that the Athenians themselves were not entirely clear on these points. For example, the plight of the grandson who delivered Isaios VIII (which will be treated below) shows that the rules were far from unambiguous. Adoption of a daughter's son may well have been intended as a consolidation of the position of the adoptee and as a safeguard of his mother's present marriage, in addition to its usual function as a means of ensuring the continuation of the adopter's οἶκος.

Even so, there are certain indications that a legitimate grandson would usually be considered the heir of his maternal grandfather, if the latter had left no male offspring, even in those cases where he had been born in a marriage contracted by ἐγγύη. The first argument in favour of this assumption is that inheritance could be transmitted through female *collateral* heirs to their descendants. This was the case when e.g. Makartatos' sister "inherited" from her two childless brothers[20], and likewise when Apollodoros Eupolidou's sisters had his property awarded to them as recorded in Isaios VII.31. None of these women had

---

[18] Wyse (1904) expressed some doubt to this effect (p.352 and pp.608sq., and Gernet (1921) argued directly against this theory (p. 351 with n.1.), followed by Erdmann (1934) pp.75sq. U.E. Paoli (1946) argued that a descendant would always exclude a collateral, and inferred from this that collateral relatives lost their right to claim the ἐπίκληρος in marriage, if she had already had a son in her marriage contracted by ἐγγύη. But even those scholars who, in more recent investigations, base their argumentation on the traditional view are forced to admit that there is no decisive evidence, as e.g. Schaps (1979), p.28, Harrison (1968) p.12 and pp.309-311, and Just (1989), pp.96sq.
[19] As suggested e.g. by Wyse (1904), p.609.
[20] Isaios XI.49.

been the object of an ἐπιδικασία. It may therefore be assumed *a fortiori* that inheritance could be transmitted through female *descendants* to their sons, even if these sons had been born in a marriage contracted by ἐγγύη. A number of cases known from the orators, and one fictional case invented by Menander may corroborate this assumption.

1) In the case presented in Isaios X we find a grandson claiming the inheritance left by his maternal grandfather. His mother had not been the object of an ἐπιδικασία, but had been married to a man outside her father's ἀγχιστεία. Her father's relatives had possessed themselves of his inheritance and had carried out a posthumous adoption. It was only after the death of the posthumously adopted son that the grandson advanced his claim. By then, thirty-seven years had passed since the collaterals took possession of the inheritance, but the speaker explains this long period of passivity by the fact that he had been an ἄτιμος as a public debtor[21]. The fact that the speaker did after all claim the inheritance of his grandfather in spite of the fact that he had been born in a marriage contracted by ἐγγύη shows, at least, that he was not *unambiguously* excluded as an heir by the legislation.

2) In Isaios VIII.40 there is a reference to the fate of three sisters which in some respects resembles that of the speaker's mother in Isaios X. The uterine half-brother of these sisters had, according to the speaker, got himself posthumously adopted as the son of his stepfather, the girls' father. Later the husbands of two of the sisters tried to claim the inheritance on behalf of their wives. There is no suggestion that they would at the same time be prepared to jeopardise their marriages, but, on the other hand, the description in Isaios VIII is so brief and so partial that a reconstruction of the actual development of the case is hardly possible[22].

3) In Dem. XXVIII.1-7, Demosthenes tries to prove that his maternal grandfather, Gylon, had not been a public debtor at his death. This argument served to counter the allegation made by his opponent, Aphobos, that Demosthenes' father had wished to conceal his property from the public authorities in order to prevent the debt from being recovered from his estate. Now, Gylon's only descendants were two daughters who had both been given in marriage while he himself was

---

[21] Isaios X.20: ἐμοί τι ἀτύχημα πρὸς τὸ δημόσιον συνέβη.
[22] The speaker recounts how the adopted son, Diokles, who was nicknamed "Orestes", met the claims of the husbands with violence and even murder. Cf. Isaios frg. VIII (Baiter & Sauppe) which was written against Diokles, possibly in a γραφὴ ὕβρεως.

still alive, one of them to Demosthenes' father. The fact that the debt would pass to the daughters' sons proves *e contrario* that they were considered the lawful heirs of their maternal grandfathers, although their mothers had been married by ἐγγύη.

4) In Menander's *Aspis*, vv.270-273, Smikrines refuses to let his niece marry the young man who is in love with her, even though he was being given the chance to keep the property that went with her. His reason for this refusal is that the sons who would be born to his niece from her marriage would later be in a position to claim the inheritance and force Smikrines to give it up to them. Smikrines' argument is perhaps the best indication that grandsons born in marriages contracted by ἐγγύη could inherit from their maternal grandfathers.

5) Isaios VIII is a speech delivered by a man who claimed the inheritance of his maternal grandfather. His mother had predeceased her father and, for this reason, had never been the object of an ἐπιδικασία. Of course, the fact that her son claimed her father's inheritance anyway does not prove that he had a better claim than his opponent, a nephew of the deceased. The speaker presents a very technical argument in (30-34) in order to prove that a descendant had a better claim than collaterals, even if his descent was through a woman who had never been the object of an ἐπιδικασία. Not surprisingly, it was precisely this speech which aroused Wyse's scepticism as to the position of a daughter's son in those cases where the daughter had not been married by ἐπιδικασία. On the other hand, it need not be doubted that the laws regulating inheritance *could* be interpreted in the way suggested by the speaker, especially when considering the four cases presented above.

Nonetheless, this speech illustrates the fact that the position of a daughter's son was indeed insecure when it came to claiming the inheritance of his maternal grandfather. The fact that the speaker in question did not take possession of the inheritance right away without prior ἐπιδικασία is quite important in this respect. He could probably have barred the ἐπιδικασία by means of a διαμαρτυρία. A διαμαρτυρία was issued on behalf of Pyrrhos' daughter Phile stating that she was a legitimate descendant of Pyrrhos whose inheritance was therefore not ἐπίδικος. The result of this move was that Phile's husband, who had delivered the διαμαρτυρία, was prosecuted in a δίκη ψευδομαρτυρίων which he lost, probably because his opponent succeeded in proving that Phile was illegitimate. Nevertheless, his course of action shows that it was not only male descendants who employed διαμαρτυρία to bar ἐπιδικασίαι. Why did the speaker of Isaios VIII choose not to? A possible answer is that there was a risk connected with the διαμαρτυρία. The person employing this procedure had to be confident that his oath would be accepted: he had to pay a deposit (παρακαταβολή) amounting to 10% of the inheritance[23], and this would probably prevent a claimant from barring an ἐπιδικασία by this means if his position was ambiguous.

We do not know of any Athenian who employed this procedure in connection with his maternal grandfather's inheritance. It is not inconceivable that some did, but the risk would have to be assessed in each individual case, where each grandson would have to judge for himself his chances of success. As often in connection with the working of Athenian law it is perhaps misleading to think of "rights" as opposed to "legitimate claims" in the absolute sense of "the right to employ a διαμαρτυρία".

The law that no one was to possess an inheritance without prior ἐπιδικασία did not apply to descendants. In this respect, we may say that they had a "right of ἐμβάτευσις". When a descendant found himself in a situation where his privileged position was being challenged by rival claimants, he had a procedural means of barring ἐπιδικασίαι, namely the διαμαρτυρία, which was not available to collateral heirs, but counter-procedures were available to collaterals who wanted to maintain their claims, and each person would have to weigh the pros and cons for himself before employing them. An obvious risk for a grandson would be that his opponents might claim that he or his mother was illegitimate, but it is equally possible, bearing in mind the passage from Isaios VIII.30 sqq., that a jury might be persuaded that a grandson was not entitled to possess the inheritance of his maternal grandfather without prior ἐπιδικασία.

We may now return to the question asked at the beginning of this section, namely whether collaterals could demand that the marriage of an ἐπίκληρος be dissolved if she had already given birth to a son. I would suggest that it is not inconceivable that her son, or another person on his behalf, would sometimes or even often succeed in fending off his relatives by means of a διαμαρτυρία, if he was prepared to run the risk.

---

[23] Pollux VIII.39 is the only evidence for this percentage in private law-suits. See Harrison (1971), p.180.

But we know no actual cases where this had happened, so the question cannot be answered with certainty.

However, it is quite clear that the position of a grandson born in a marriage contracted by ἐγγύη vis-à-vis the relatives of his maternal grandfather was often insecure, even if he had a better claim than any collateral heir to his grandfather's inheritance *qua* his legitimate descendant. So although adoption was not absolutely necessary for a grandfather who wanted to make sure that his grandson would succeed to his property as his heir, adoption might still be an effective means of preventing difficulties from arising after his death. It is perhaps significant in this regard that the speaker of Isaios VIII found it worthwhile to explain in detail why his maternal grandfather had *not* adopted him[24]. He may have expected the jury to interpret this fact as evidence for his mother's having been born out of wedlock. At the same time, this is an indication that adoption of grandsons was not uncommon. We may count them as adoptions of intestate heirs in spite of the fact that the position of a grandson was not always unambiguous; after all, the son of an only daughter could be seen as the lawful descendant and heir of his maternal grandfather, as indicated by the cases referred to above. And since a grandfather would have other means at his disposal by which he could secure both his daughter's marriage and his grandson's position, such as a will not providing for adoption, we may still interpret the five recorded adoptions of grandsons as testifying to the importance attached to the artificial continuation of a family-line which would otherwise have become extinct.

---

[24] Isaios VIII.36.

Chapter 6: Posthumous adoption and intestate heirs

In the preceding chapter it has been argued that adoption was not an obligatory supplement to the ἐπίκληρος-institution, and that the decision to continue the οἶκος of the ἐπίκληρος' father rested entirely with his heirs. But there is one more piece of evidence which has to be considered, before this conclusion can be drawn, and that is the allegation made in Isaios VII.30:
"All those who are about to die make their own precautions so that their οἶκοι will not become empty, and so that there will be someone to offer sacrifices at their tombs and perform all the customary rites for them. Wherefore, even if they are to die childless, they do in any case leave adopted children. And it is not only private individuals who make this decision; it is also a decision of public concern made by the πόλις as a community. For it (the πόλις) orders by law the Archon to take care of the οἶκοι so that they do not become empty". (πάντες γὰρ οἱ τελευτήσειν μέλλοντες πρόνοιαν ποιοῦνται σφῶν αὐτῶν, ὅπως μὴ ἐξερημώσουσι τοὺς σφετέρους αὐτῶν οἴκους, ἀλλ' ἔσται τις [καὶ] ὁ ἐναγιῶν καὶ πάντα τὰ νομιζόμενα αὐτοῖς ποιήσων· διὸ κἂν ἄπαιδες τελευτήσωσιν, ἀλλ' οὖν ποιησάμενοι καταλείπουσι. Καὶ οὐ μόνον ἰδίᾳ ταῦτα γιγνώσκουσιν, ἀλλὰ καὶ δημοσίᾳ τὸ κοινὸν τῆς πόλεως οὕτω ταῦτ' ἔγνωκε· νόμῳ γὰρ τῷ ἄρχοντι τῶν οἴκων, ὅπως ἂν μὴ ἐξερημῶνται, προστάττει τὴν ἐπιμέλειαν.)

This is the only source we have for the view that adoption was indeed the concern of the entire community, and that the community as such took active measures to guarantee the artificial continuation of family-lines which would otherwise become extinct. Some scholars have taken this allegation at face value[1], and have inferred that the law provided

---

[1] E.Caillemer (1879) pp.132sqq. interprets the law to the effect that the Archon had to find a citizen who would "take the place of the deceased" in those cases where no members of the latter's ἀγχιστεία had advanced a claim on the inheritance. Lipsius (1905-15) is sceptical as to the value of the passage, partly because there is no additional evidence to support the claim of the speaker of Isaios VII (see esp.p.509, n.30), but he offers no alternative interpretation. Nonetheless, he interprets [Dem.] XLIII.75 as a manifestation of "das interesse, das auch der Staat daran hatte, insbesondere leistungsfähige Häuser nicht aussterben zu lassen". See Harrison (1968) p.92 n.1 for other references to the discussion. Harrison himself does not take a firm stand on this matter, although he expresses his doubts as to whether the Archon could in fact force a collateral heir to carry out a posthumous adoption in the IV. century (*ibid.* pp.92sq.).

for the active intervention by the Archon, whose task it was to ensure that family-lines were perpetuated by means of posthumous adoption.

The allegation made by the speaker of Isaios VII gives rise to at least two central questions, namely 1) whether an intestate heir was under any legal obligations to continue the οἶκος of a childless deceased, and 2), if not, whether the passage from Isaios VII is to be interpreted as evidence that there was a strong moral obligation to carry out posthumous adoptions and that an intestate heir would be exposed to considerable social pressure from his surroundings.

1. Posthumous adoption - a legal obligation?

In [Dem.] XLIII.75 a law is quoted, and its wording is in fact very close to the wording of the paraphrase made by the speaker of Isaios VII: "The Archon is to look after orphans, ἐπίκληροι, those οἶκοι which are becoming empty, and those women who remain in the οἶκοι of their deceased husbands, claiming to be pregnant. He shall look after them and not allow anyone to commit outrages in respect to these". (Ὁ ἄρχων ἐπιμελείσθω τῶν ὀρφανῶν καὶ τῶν ἐπικλήρων καὶ τῶν οἴκων τῶν ἐξερημουμένων καὶ τῶν γυναικῶν, ὅσαι μένουσιν ἐν τοῖς οἴκοις τῶν ἀνδρῶν τῶν τεθνηκότων φάσκουσαι κυεῖν. τούτων ἐπιμελείσθω καὶ μὴ ἐάτω ὑβρίζειν μηδένα περὶ τούτους). It cannot be determined with absolute certainty whether the law quoted in [Dem.] XLIII.75 is in fact the law referred to by the speaker of Isaios VII, or whether we are dealing with two different laws.

It must be noted, however, that the line of argument in [Dem.] XLIII which the law-quotation is supposed to corroborate is remarkably similar to the argument in Isaios VII.30: "So, I managed our affairs in this way in order for the οἶκοι of Bouselos' descendants to be preserved as far as possible. I shall examine these again. And first, read out this law here." (ἐγὼ μὲν οὖν τοῦτον τὸν τρόπον διῴκησα, ὅπως ἂν διασῴζωνται ὅτι μάλιστα οἱ οἶκοι οἱ ἀπὸ Βουσέλου· τούτους δὲ ἐξετάσωμεν πάλιν. Καὶ πρώτιστον μὲν τὸν νόμον τουτονὶ ἀνάγνωθι.) Having had the law on the Archon's obligations read out, the speaker resumes his argument in (76): "How could people be more sure to cause an οἶκος to be deserted..." followed by a description of the conduct of his opponents.

Apparently, both the speaker of Isaios VII and the speaker of [Dem.] XLIII interpret the law on the Archon's obligations as regards deserted οἶκοι as a legal measure taken to prevent the extinction of family-lines.

The law-text itself does not prove that the Archon was required to induce or force intestate heirs to carry out posthumous adoptions. It only states that he was to "look after" those οἶκοι which were becoming empty and prevent any attempt to outrage them or to commit legal offences in respect to them. A typical legal offence committed in respect to the οἶκος of a man who left no male offspring would be to seize it without prior ἐπιδικασία[2]. But was it in any way considered a legal offence to leave the οἶκος of a childless deceased empty, and was the Archon expected to intervene if this happened[3]?

I have found no instances of the Archon having initiated a procedure of posthumous adoption. This is in itself no proof that it did not happen, since most of our known examples of posthumous are alleged to have been illegal anyway. But even in the two allegedly legal cases known to us, we know that the Archon had not been involved at any stage. It is safe to infer *e silentio* that the posthumous adoption of Euboulides III had not been initiated or sanctioned by the Archon, because, if it had been, the speaker of [Dem.] XLIII who based his argument on the validity of the adoption would have helped his cause by mentioning this fact. Furthermore, in Isaios XI Theopompos tries to justify his having initiated a posthumous adoption. By this adoption his son, Makartatos II, had been transferred to the οἶκος of his maternal uncle, Makartatos I, who had been Theopompos' brother-in-law. Theopompos claims that the adoption took place at the request of his wife, Makartatos I's sister[4], and not because the Archon had in any way prompted him to do so.

---

[2] Cf. the law quoted in [Dem.] XLVI.22: ἀνεπίδικον δὲ κλῆρον μὴ ἔχειν. This was Wyse's interpretation of the law (1904, p.576), followed by MacDowell (1989) pp.1-21, esp. p.19, where he argues that the word οἶκος only acquired its meaning of "family" in the V. century.

[3] The law-text leaves it at the Archon's discretion to impose fines "according to the fixed rate" (MacDowell's translation (1978, p.236). In those cases where the Archon found that an offence was to be met with a sanction which would exceed the limit of 50 dr. "having summoned the offender five days in advance and stated the penalty (on the writ of summons?) according to what he sees fit, he is to take the case to the People's Court" (προσκαλεσάμενος πρόπεμπτα καὶ τίμημα ἐπιγραψάμενος, ὅ τι ἂν δοκῇ αὐτῷ, εἰσαγέτω εἰς τὴν ἡλιαίαν). MacDowell holds that the Archon had to act as prosecutor when bringing the case to court (1978, p.237), thus taking the initiative which would normally be the rôle of ὁ βουλόμενος (but see Hansen, 1981).

[4] Isaios XI.49: ἐπείσθην ὑπ' ἐκείνης εἰσποιῆσαι Μακαρτάτῳ τὸν ἕτερον τῶν παίδων·

Again, this only goes to show that the Archon would not normally have been involved in posthumous adoptions: it still does not prove that he was not required to intervene, if the intestate heirs failed to carry them out. But we know of several instances of intestate heirs neglecting to continue the οἶκος of the deceased by means of posthumous adoption. In Isaios VII.31 the speaker claims that his opponent had not made sure that the οἶκος of her deceased brother would be continued. This is a strong indication that it was entirely up to the intestate heirs to initiate posthumous adoptions, and that there was no centralised attempt to guarantee that it would indeed happen. Likewise, in [Dem.] XLIII.78, Makartatos is blamed for not having carried out a posthumous adoption in order to perpetuate Hagnias' line. In [Dem.] XLVIII, there are no hints at all that Olympiodoros ever thought of continuing Komon's οἶκος; what is more, the issue is not even touched on by his opponent, who might, one would have thought, have stood to gain from blackening his opponent's character by pointing out his negligence to the judges. But it is quite clear from this speech that failing to carry out a posthumous adoption on the part of the intestate heirs would not give rise to legal sanctions, and that the decision to initiate a posthumous adoption rested with the heirs themselves, not with the Archon.

This conclusion may be corroborated by referring to the law which is quoted in [Dem.] XLIII.16. The law concerns the reopening of inheritance-cases by means of new ἐπιδικασίαι. New claimants were allowed to advance their claims until five years after the death of the person who had held the inheritance as a result of a previous ἐπιδικασία.

Now, if a posthumous adoption had been carried out by the heir who had had the inheritance awarded to him in a previous ἐπιδικασία, then the inheritance was no longer ἐπίδικος, and the adopted son would have procedural means of barring subsequent attempts to instigate new ἐπιδικασίαι. Therefore, it is very unlikely that the law concerning the reopening of inheritance-suits could have existed side by side with regulations that obliged the intestate heirs to provide for posthumous adoptions. If the heirs had been under any legal obligation to continue the οἶκος of the deceased, the law which warranted new ἐπιδικασίαι would never come into operation, unless the intestate heirs had omitted to do what was in fact their duty.

All points to the conclusion that it was not considered illegal in IV. century Athens to allow a family-line to become extinct, and that the

Archon did not actually intervene to prompt the heirs to carry out posthumous adoptions. But if the Isaios-passage is, nevertheless, to be interpreted to the effect that, legally, the Archon was required to see to it that posthumous adoptions did indeed take place, it must be concluded that we are dealing with a regulation which was ignored in practice in IV. century Athens. The existence of such a regulation was incompatible with the law permitting renewed ἐπιδικασίαι.

2. Posthumous adoption - a moral obligation?

Some of the passages referred to above under point 1) may be taken to indicate that the intestate heirs were, to a certain extent, considered morally obliged to carry out posthumous adoptions. Thrasyllos, the speaker of Isaios VII, claims that his opponent had acted αἰσχρῶς and δεινῶς by allowing her brother's οἶκος to become empty[5]. And Sositheos, in [Dem.] XLIII.77, brands Makartatos as ὑβριστής for having omitted to continue Hagnias' line. Presumably, both speakers hoped to rouse the judges' indignation at the negligence and impiety shown by their opponents. Even so, it still has to be decided whether the moral obligation was so strong that only the most unscrupulous collateral heir would venture not to perform a posthumous adoption.

It has been pointed out in chapter 4 that intestate heirs do not normally refer to their own prospective duties concerning the tomb-cult of the deceased, not even in those speeches delivered with the aim of having an adoption rejected by the People's Court. Nor do they normally mention posthumous adoption as a possibility. The only exception is the speaker of [Dem.] XLIV who proclaims that a posthumously adopted son is to continue the οἶκος of Archiades instead of Leochares, if the speaker should succeed in having the latter's adoption overruled by the People's Court[6]. But, in general, it does not seem as if the collateral heirs expected to be able to win the favour of the judges by showing their willingness to carry out posthumous adoptions.

---

[5] Isaios VII.31, cf. ibid.44.
[6] [Dem.] XLIV.43, 66.

In all the extant speeches in which collateral heirs attack the validity of testamentary adoptions, there is not a single reference to the possibility of adopting posthumously. This silence may be interpreted in two ways. One possible interpretation is that posthumous adoption was considered a matter of course. For this reason, the collateral heirs did not consider it worthwhile to spend their limited time on pointing out to the judges what was in fact obvious. Another interpretation is that collateral heirs were not generally expected to provide for posthumous adoptions. The heirs did not expect that the considerations extending to the preservation of the οἶκος of the deceased would have any influence on the judges' decision.

In favour of the second interpretation is first and foremost the fact that it would not have been all collaterals who could reasonably be expected to carry out a posthumous adoption. In Isaios II.10, the speaker claims that it would have been 'disgraceful' (αἰσχρόν), if Menekles had adopted his brother's only son and thus had continued his own οἶκος at the expense of that of his brother. If it could be claimed that it was wrong for a citizen to continue his οἶκος at the expense of another, it is not likely that a collateral heir would be expected to let himself be adopted posthumously in those cases where the adoption would jeopardise the οἶκος of his natural father.

Moreover, it was not uncommon for childless Athenians to adopt heirs who, already before the adoption, had the best claim to their inheritance. The relatively high frequency of this type of adoptions is hardly in keeping with the assumption that posthumous adoption was expected from the intestate heirs. If a childless man, or a man who had daughters only, could be sure that his heirs would provide for an adoption, adopting without disrupting the order of intestate succession would seem somewhat superfluous.

It must therefore be excluded that posthumous adoption was regarded as a matter of course. The reason why the collateral heirs do not mention posthumous adoption as a possibility in their lawcourt speeches is then more likely to have been that the judges were not expected to let this issue have any influence on their decision as to who was to inherit. It is thus quite remarkable that a claimant who wanted to challenge the validity of an adoption did not find it necessary or even advantageous to stress his own willingness to provide a descendant for the οἶκος of the deceased, who would take the place of the adopted son under attack.

But some categories of intestate heirs may have been under a stronger moral obligation to provide for posthumous adoptions than others. In Isaios VII.32, the speaker argues *a fortiori*: the intestate heirs of Apollodoros had not taken pains to see to the continuation of the οἶκος of their very own brother. How could Apollodoros, then, expect them to provide a posthumously adopted son for himself, as he was but their cousin? Although this kind of rhetorical logic must be taken with (at least) a grain of salt when used as evidence, the speaker's reasoning is based on the assumption that the moral obligation tended to be stronger, the closer the relationship between the deceased and his heirs. There is other evidence which points to the same conclusion, namely the two, possibly three testamentary adoptions of women, which would indicate that the testators expected a prospective son of their adopted daughters to be transferred to their οἶκοι by posthumous adoption. Perhaps the strongest moral obligation was in fact incumbent on the male descendants of an ἐπίκληρος to continue the family-line of their maternal grandfather. But the evidence does not warrant a safe conclusion to this effect: a testator may have included as an additional provision in his will that a son of his adopted daughter was later to be posthumously adopted. Also, as has been pointed out in chapter 5, it was not uncommon for grandfathers to provide for adoptions of their daughters' sons, while they themselves were still alive, which indicates to the contrary that they could not be sure that their family-lines would indeed be continued.

Finally it must be pointed out that posthumous adoption was not always construed as an act of piety. This may be exemplified by Theopompos' line of argument in Isaios XI.49sq. Here Theopompos attempts to prove that he did not get his son adopted posthumously into the οἶκος of Makartatos I simply in order to avoid the burden of liturgies himself. Theopompos seems to anticipate an allegation by his opponents that he would have been liable to liturgies if Makartatos' property had been added to what he already possessed. For because of the posthumous adoption, the inheritance left by Makartatos would not be counted as part of Theopompos' property. Apparently, Theopompos expected his opponents to hold this adoption against him as a way of blackening his character along the lines of: "See how he shirks liturgical burdens!"

What is interesting here is that Theopompos does not try to counter his opponents by turning their argument to his own advantage. He does not use the posthumous adoption to prove that he was indeed a "model citizen" who had acted in a way expected from any decent person responsible for the fate of a dying οἶκος. On the contrary, he was "persuaded by his wife" into carrying out the adoption (rather ironically, if we bear in mind the wording of the Solonic law on διατίθεσθαι τὰ ἑαυτοῦ). Now, if posthumous adoption had in fact been generally recognised as a strong moral obligation incumbent on intestate heirs, would it have been necessary for Theopompos to defend this action in the way he does?[7]

The conclusion of this chapter is that posthumous adoption was not always expected from the intestate heirs of a childless deceased in the IV. century. There was no legal obligation to carry out posthumous adoptions, and the moral obligation was far from strong enough to allow the assumption that most intestate heirs would provide for such an adoption - for moral reasons alone, at any rate.

---

[7] Cf. the line of argument in [Dem.] XLIII.11-13, where the speaker conflates the instrumental aspects of the posthumous adoption in question (...ἀλλ' ἡγούμενος εἰκός τι παθεῖν τοὺς τότε δικάζοντας, 11) with the pious aspects of the act.

Chapter 7: Conclusion

The Athenian laws that applied to adoption and inheritance in general do not at all suggest that the Athenians considered their institution of adoption a means of achieving an ultimate political goal: to keep a stable number of κλῆροι by preventing the division or amalgamation of property otherwise inevitable in an inheritance-system that did not recognise primogeniture. The only known law that may possibly be interpreted as a centralized attempt, on the part of the πόλις, to prevent the Athenian οἶκοι from becoming extinct is the law discussed in chapter 6, which defined the duties of the Archon. It was the duty of the Archon "to look after those οἶκοι which were becoming empty", and this law was quoted already by Fustel de Coulanges, and later by a number of his successors, in support of the view that the all-embracing πόλις took an active interest in securing the continuation of its individual οἶκοι, for religious as well as for fiscal reasons. But whatever the original intentions of this law, it is clear that, in the IV. century, it was not considered the duty of the Archon to intervene in order to ensure that empty οἶκοι would be continued by means of adoption, and it is indeed doubtful whether the law had ever operated in this way.

At least in the IV. century, this interpretation of the law would come into conflict with the law permitting the re-opening of ἐπιδικασίαι. The latter took into account only those cases where the intestate heirs in possession had not provided for posthumous adoption; for if a posthumous adoption *had* in fact been carried out, the adoptee would be in a position to bar any attempt made by rival claimants to re-open the inheritance-suit, as shown in chapter 3. We know several examples of inheritance-suits that were re-opened (most notorious are the suits concerning the inheritance left by Hagnias), whereas there is no trace in our sources of the Archon's having played an active part in preventing a family-line from becoming extinct.

Similarly, the legislation on ἐπίκληροι and the rights of their descendants did not contain any provisions concerning adoption. The only known requirement that had to be met before the son of an ἐπίκληρος was allowed to take possession of the inheritance left by his maternal grandfather was one of age.

It is also worth noting that the law which regulated intestate succession did not contain any provisions designed to increase the frequency of adoption. The law gave the closest relative(s) first priority, unconditionally. In this respect it was considered irrelevant whether or not it would be possible for the closest relative to carry out a posthumous adoption without jeopardizing the continuation of the οἶκος of his natural father.

Thus, it rested entirely with each individual citizen to take the initiative, if an adoption was to be carried out. Apparently, no attempt was made to encourage the Athenians to adopt, although the Athenians certainly recognised adoption as a legal institution. This is evident from the laws that defined the rights and obligations of an adoptee, such as the law that limited his right to return to the οἶκος of his natural father, and the law that guaranteed his right to an equal share in the inheritance left by the adopter, even if the latter had begotten natural sons after the adoption.

However, as a legal institution, adoption was controlled first and foremost locally, by the phratries and demes. As has been argued in chapter 3, posthumous adoption, as well as adoption *inter vivos*, could be carried out without reference to the People's Court or any magistrate. It was the recognition of the adoptee by the adopter's phratry and deme that constituted the adoption and conferred the status of descendant on the adoptee. It was only in connection with testamentary adoption that the sanction of the People's Court was obligatory, because the testamentary heir did not yet have the rights of a descendant at the death of the testator. Once the will had been accepted and the adoptee recognised by the phratry and deme of the testator, the adoptee had exactly the same rights and obligations as those who had been adopted *inter vivos* or posthumously. What was decided by the People's Court was only whether he had the best claim to the inheritance by virtue of the will as opposed to by virtue of kinship, that is, whether the will was to be accepted as genuine and legal. This also means that the information given in the Aristotelian *Problemata* 950b, that judges tended to vote in favour of kinship rather than wills, does not necessarily indicate a hostile attitude to testamentary *adoption*, but only to the nature of the written document that warranted it, a document that could easily have been faked.

If we accept that the most important task of the People's Court was to decide, not on the question of whether adoption should be carried out at all, but on whether a particular will or adoption *inter vivos* was in accordance with the laws, this would account for the curious difference in arguments used by adoptees and intestate heirs respectively, whenever they ended up as opponents in court. Adopted sons would gain from stressing the importance of the institution in general terms; indeed, it was an indispensable argument if they were to argue for the plausibility of their own adoptions. They had to focus on the plight of a childless old age, on the importance of annual commemoration at the tomb of the adopter, on the disaster of leaving one's οἶκος empty. The intestate heirs passed over these points in silence. Apparently, it was quite sufficient if they could prove that their opponent had not been legally adopted, or that the will, on which he based his claim, was a fake or had been written in a fit of rage or while the testator had been under the influence of a woman, etc. Even so, it would seem that the "ordinary Athenian", as represented by judges in the People's Court, showed a remarkable lack of interest in the fate of the οἶκος of his fellow-citizen. Apart from the speaker of [Dem] XLIV, none of the intestate heirs seems to have expected the issue of posthumous adoption to carry any weight with the judges. It might have been imagined that one of the more efficient ways of countering the stock-arguments of an adopted opponent would be for the intestate heir to stress his own willingness to replace the adoptee by means of posthumous adoption. But, apparently, this was not the case. Is it that we are, after all, dealing with an institution that was on the wane in the IV. century?

Not necessarily. The Athenians' seeming lack of interest in other people's οἶκοι (if we are to judge from the relatively few extant speeches concerning inheritance) may simply be due to the fact that adoption was seen as a purely individual concern and not as the concern of the entire community. If a childless man wanted to adopt, or if his relatives wanted to carry out an adoption on his behalf, well and good, as long as the adoption was in accordance with the laws. This last point was the crucial one when the case was disputed in court, and it is perfectly possible to imagine that an Athenian who had just voted against an adoption in an inheritance-suit would answer, if asked, that he himself would naturally adopt a son if faced with the prospect of a childless old age and deprivation of annual commemorative rites, only *his* adoption would of course be legal and beyond reproach.

Furthermore, adoption was optional when drawing up a will, as argued in chapter 4; yet at least seven of the 17 known wills drawn up by men without natural sons can be said with certainty to have contained provisions on adoption, while an additional five may possibly have included such provisions. There is every reason to believe that these wills reflect a genuine wish, on the part of the testators, to leave an heir behind who would take upon himself the responsibility of a descendant. That adoption in IV. century Athens was more than just an empty formality, a survival from an earlier (archaic) age, may be further corroborated by the epigraphical evidence that shows that the institution was still alive and kicking in Hellenistic and even Roman Athens (see my compilation of inscriptions in Rubinstein et al.:1991).

The evidence of the Attic Orators for the institution of adoption does not warrant the conclusion that the IV. century was a phase of transition during which the archaic and classical concept of the family was changing radically. It does not prove the existence of the postulated gap (which has then been bridged by means of the same body of textual evidence) between the Athenian "other", the archaic age, and the Athenians of the Hellenistic age who have been alleged to have resembled "us", being utterly rational, individualistic, and secular. On the contrary, if we are to judge from the Athenian way of practising adoption in the IV. century, the evidence points to continuity rather than change.

Catalogue of attested adoptions

a) Adoptions *inter vivos*

cat.no. 1 ref.: [Dem.]XLIV.19,46
type of adoption: probably *inter vivos*. The speaker claims in (19) that the adoption had been posthumous, but he contradicts himself in (46): ὁ γὰρ 'Αρχιάδης...ἐποιήσατο υἱὸν τὸν τοῦ διαμεμαρτυρηκότος νυνὶ πάππον, which indicates an adoption *inter vivos*, cf.61.
adopter: 'Αρχιάδης Εὐθυμάχου 'Οτρυνεύς (9) (PA 2441)
adoptee: Λεωκράτης (PA 9088)
natural father of adoptee: ? 'Ελευσίνιος
relationship by blood between adopter and adoptee: Leokrates was the son of Archiades' sister's daughter (17)
Was the adoption challenged? no (19-20)
Date: ?

cat.no. 2 ref. Dem. XLI.3-5
type of adoption: *inter vivos*
adopter: Πολύευκτος Τειθράσιος (PA 11944, Hesp. VI, p.341)
adoptee: Λεωκράτης (PA 9090)
natural father of adoptee: ?
relationship by blood between adopter and adoptee: (?)Leokrates was the brother-in-law of Polyeuktos
Was the adoption challenged? no, it was cancelled by Polyeuktos himself
Date: ? Blass (1898), pp.251 sq.) dates Dem.XLI to an early stage in Demosthenes' production, but the adoption may have taken place long before the speech was delivered.

cat.no. 3 ref. Isaios II *pass*.
type of adoption: *inter vivos* (14)
adopter: Μενεκλῆς (PA 9906)
adoptee: ?
natural father of adoptee: Ἐπώνυμος 'Αχαρνεύς (3) (PA 5020)
relationship by blood between adopter and adoptee: none. Menekles had been married to the adoptee's sister, but had divorced her. (5-10)
Was the adoption challenged? yes, by Menekles' brother (24)
Procedure: δίκη ψευδομαρτυρίων (2,17,24)
Date: Isaios II cannot be dated with certainty, but it is normally placed in the 350's (Wyse (1904), pp. 236sq.) In that case the adoption must have taken place in the 380's or early 370's.

cat.no. 4 ref. Isaios VII *pass*.
type of adoption: *inter vivos* (1)
adopter: 'Απολλόδωρος Θρασύλλου (5) (PA 1395)
adoptee: Θράσυλλος (17,27)
natural father of adoptee: ?
relationship by blood between adopter and adoptee: Thrasyllos was the son of Apollodoros' uterine half-sister
Was the adoption challenged? yes, by the daughter of Apollodoros' uncle, his father's brother (18)
Procedure: διαδικασία (1-3)
Date: Isaios VII is dated to ca. 355 B.C. (Wyse (1904), p.549: after 357/6, Wankel, (1988), pp.199sqq. *pace* Ruschenbusch (1987) and (1991), who dates the speech to 354)

cat.no. 5   ref. [Plut.]*Vit. X Orat.* 838sq.
type of adoption: *inter vivos*   Dio.Hal.*Isocr.* 18
adopter: Ἰσοκράτης Θεοδώρου Ἐρχιεύς
adoptee: Ἀφάρευς
natural father of adoptee: Ἱππίας (839B)
relationship by blood between adopter and adoptee: Aphareus was a son born to
                                                        Isokrates' wife, Plathane, in a previous marriage
Was the adoption challenged? no
Date: before Isokrates' death in 338. He was old when he adopted Aphareus (838A)

b) Testamentary adoptions

(* indicates that it is not stated explicitly in the sources that the beneficiary was in fact adopted.)

cat.no. 6*   ref. Isaios I *pass*.
type of adoption: possibly testamentary, but it is not stated explicitly that Kleonymos adopted any of his beneficiaries. It is indeed possible that his will did not provide for adoption.
testator: Κλεώνυμος Πολυάρχου (4) (PA 8681)
adoptee: ? Φερένικος (31) (PA 14198)
natural father of adoptee: ?
relationship by blood between adopter and adoptee: It appear from (6) that K. was related by blood to his beneficiary (or beneficiaries) in some way, but no details are given.
Was the adoption challenged? yes, by Kleonymos' nephews (4)
Procedure: probably διαδικασία
Date: Isaios I cannot be dated with any certainty

cat.no. 7   ref. Isaios III *pass*.
type of adoption: testamentary (1,56)
testator: Πύρρος (1) (PA 12506)
adoptee: Ἔνδιος (1) (PA 4702)
natural father of adoptee: ?
relationship by blood between adopter and adoptee: Endios was the son of Pyrrhos'
                                                          sister (1)
Was the adoption challenged? no, at least not in Endios' lifetime (1)
Date: Isaios III cannot be dated with any certainty

cat.no. 8   ref. Isaios V *pass*.
type of adoption: testamentary (6, 14-15)
testator: Δικαιογένης Μενεξένου Κυδαθηναιεύς (5) (PA 3775)
adoptee: Δικαιογένης (6) (PA 3774)
natural father of adoptee: Πρόξενος Ἀφιδναῖος (6) (PA 12267)
relationship by blood between adopter and adoptee: It is normally assumed that Dikaiogenes adopted the (grand?)son of his father's sister (cf. Davies *APF* p.476), but there is no evidence to corroborate this assumption, apart from the fact that adopter and adoptee had the same name.
Was the adoption challenged? yes. Apparently, the relatives of Dikaiogenes first accepted his will as genuine (6), but later his sisters' sons challenged the position of the adoptee by instigating an ἐπιδικασία. This was met with a διαμαρτυρία by Leochares on behalf of the adoptee. (16)
Procedure: see above. The sons of the adopter's sisters instigated a δίκη ψευδομαρτυρίων against Leochares but dropped the suit just before the votes of the judges were to be counted (16-17).
Date: Dikaiogenes M. K. died in 411

cat.no. 9*   **ref.** Isaios VII.9
type of adoption: perhaps testamentary adoption. The testator named a husband for his beneficiary in his will, which may be interpreted to the effect that his will provided for adoption.
testator: Ἀπολλόδωρος Θρασύλλου (5) (PA 1395)
adoptee: ? (female)
natural father of adoptee: Ἀρχέδαμος (7) (PA 3212)
relationship by blood between adopter and adoptee: Apollodoros chose his uterine half-sister as his beneficiary.
Was the adoption challenged? no, as the will was probably cancelled by Apollodoros himself long before his death.
Date: Apollodoros drew up his will before joining a military expedition to Corinth, which is dated to ca.394-390 (9) (see Wyse (1904), p.557)

cat.no.10*   **ref.** Isaios X *pass*.
type of adoption: testamentary (2,22)
testator: Ἀρίσταρχος Ἀριστάρχου Συπαλήττιος (3,6) (PA 1670)
adoptee: Ξεναίνετος (1-2) (PA 11176)
natural father of adoptee: Κυρωνίδης Ξεναινέτου Ἀχαρνεύς (4-6) (PA 8950)
relationship by blood between adopter and adoptee: Xenainetos was the brother of the testator by blood, but *de jure*, the son of the testator's (paternal) uncle's daughter (4-6).
Was the adoption challenged? yes, by the son of the testator's sister by adoption. (4-6)
Procedure: probably διαδικασία
Date: Aristarchos died in the years between 378 and 371 (Wyse (1904), p.652)

cat.no.11   **ref.** Isaios IV *pass*.
type of adoption: testamentary (19)
testator: Νικόστρατος Θρασυμάχου/Σμικροῦ (3) (PA 11013)
adoptee: Χαριάδης (PA 15306)
natural father of adoptee: ?
relationship by blood between adopter and adoptee: according to Chariades' opponent they were not related by blood (18)
Was the adoption challenged? yes, by the testator's cousins ἐκ πατραδέλφου (2,23,26)
Procedure: διαδικασία (24)
Date: Nikostratos died ca. 374 (Wyse (1904), p.369)

cat.no.12*   **ref.** Isaios IV.8
type of adoption: testamentary
testator: Νικόστρατος Θρασυμάχου/Σμικροῦ (3) (PA 11013)
adoptee: Τήλεφος (PA 13574)
natural father of adoptee: ?
relationship by blood between adopter and adoptee: ?
Was the adoption challenged? The only information given in VIII.8 is the sentence "καὶ οὗτος οὐ πολλῷ ὕστερον ἐπαύσατο". Perhaps Telephos dropped his claim before the inheritance-suit had been initiated.
Date: Nikostratos died ca. 374 (Wyse (1904), p.369)

cat.no.13   ref. Isaios XI.8
type of adoption: testamentary
testator: Ἁγνίας Πολέμωνος ἐκ Οἴου ([Dem.] XLIII.23) (PA 133)
adoptee: ? (female)
natural father of adoptee: ?
relationship by blood between adopter and adoptee: The adoptee was Hagnias' niece
Was the adoption challenged? no
Date: Hagnias died either in 396 (Thompson (1976) p.14) or 370 (Humphreys (1983a)).

cat.no.14   ref. Isaios IX *pass.*
type of adoption: testamentary (2,6)
testator: Ἀστύφιλος Εὐθυκράτου Ἀραφήνιος (1,17,18,36) (PA 2665)
adoptee: NN Ἀραφήνιος
natural father of adoptee: Κλέων Θουδίππου Ἀραφήνιος (17,21) (PA 8669)
relationship by blood between adopter and adoptee: NN was by blood the son of Astyphilos' cousin, Kleon, but Kleon's father had been transferred to another οἶκος by adoption (2)
Was the adoption challenged? yes, by Astyphilos' uterine half-brother (1,27)
Procedure: probably διαδικασία
Date: ca. 369 (14)

cat.no.15   ref. Isaios VI *pass.*
type of adoption: testamentary (3,7)
testator: Φιλοκτήμων Εὐκτήμονος Κηφισιεύς (3,10) (PA 14641)
adoptee: Χαιρέστρατος (6) (IG II.2 2825.11) (PA 15164)
natural father of adoptee: Φανόστρατος Κηφισιεύς (6) (PA 14103)
relationship by blood between adopter and adoptee: Chairestratos was the son of
                                                                 Philoktemon's sister (6)
Was the adoption challenged? yes, by two boys who were claimed to be paternal half-
                                                 brothers of Philoktemon (4,10,12-14)
Procedure: the ἐπιδικασία was barred with a διαμαρτυρία delivered by Androkles on behalf of the two boys, whereupon Androkles was prosecuted with a δίκη ψευδομαρτυρίων by Chairestratos. (3-5)
Date: Isaios VI is dated by Wyse (1904) p.484, to 365/4 or 364/3

cat.no.16*   ref. Isaios XI.8sq.,
                                                                 [Dem.] XLIII.4
type of adoption: testamentary (8)
testator: Ἁγνίας Πολέμωνος ἐκ Οἴου ([Dem.] XLIII.23) (PA 133)
adoptee: Γλαύκων ([Dem.] XLIII.4, IG II.2 1742.85sq.) (PA 3004)
natural father of adoptee: Γλαυκέτης ἐξ Οἴου (IG II.2 1742.85sq.) (PA 2956)
relationship by blood between adopter and adoptee: Glaukon was Hagnias' uterine
                                                          half-brother (Isaios XI.8)
Was the adoption challenged? yes, by Phylomache who claimed that she was the daughter
                                                     of Hagnias' cousin (Isaios XI.9, [Dem.] XLIII.29)
Procedure: διαδικασία ([Dem.] XLIII.3-4)
Date: 361/0 ([Dem.] XLIII.31)

cat.no.17   ref. Isaios XI.41sq., 45
type of adoption: testamentary (41)
testator: Θεόφων (PA 7180)
adoptee: ? (female)
natural father of adoptee: Στρατοκλῆς Χαριδήμου ἐξ Οἴου ([Dem.]XLIII.42) (PA 12942)
relationship by blood between adopter and adoptee: the adoptee was the daughter of Theophon's sister (41)
Was the adoption challenged? no
Date: before 360, the earliest possible date of Isaios XI (Wyse (1904) p.677)

c1) Posthumous adoptions

cat.no.18   ref.[Dem.] XLIV *pass.*
type of adoption: posthumous (41)
adopter: Ἀρχιάδης Εὐθυμάχου Ὀτρυνεύς (9) (PA 2441)
adoptee: Λεωχάρης (41) (PA 9173)
natural father of adoptee: Λεώστρατος Λεωκράτους Ἐλευσίνιος (21-22) (PA 9154)
relationship by blood between adopter and adoptee: Leochares was the great-great-grandchild of Archiades' sister. (17,19-22)
Was the adoption challenged? yes, by the son and grandson of Archiades' brother's daughter (12-13)
Procedure: δίκη ψευδομαρτυρίων (45) in response to a διαμαρτυρία delivered by Leochares (29,42)
Date: ?

cat.no.19   ref.Isaios VIII.40sqq.
type of adoption: posthumous, according to the speaker: Isaios frgg. VIII and IX
"αὐτὸν τῷ πατρὶ αὐτῶν εἰσποιήσας, οὐδεμίαν ἐκείνου περὶ τούτων ποιησαμένου διαθήκην" (40)
adopter: ?
adoptee: Διοκλῆς Φλυεύς (Isaios VIII,3, 40sqq.) (PA 4061)
natural father of adoptee: ?
relationship by blood between adopter and adoptee: ? (Diokles was a son born from the adopter's wife in a previous marriage)
Was the adoption challenged? an attempt was allegedly made by the husbands of the adopter's daughters, but according to the speaker of Isaios VIII, Diokles retaliated by having one of them murdered and the other "walled up" (κατοικοδομήσας, 41) and managed to make him an ἄτιμος. Isaios frg. VIII was apparently delivered in this connection.
Procedure: ?
Date: Prior to the law-suit in which Isaios VIII was delivered. This speech is dated to the years 386-363 (Wyse (1904) p.588)

cat.no.20 ref.Isaios X.6,8-12, 14, 21
type of adoption: posthumous (6)
adopter: Ἀρίσταρχος Συπαλήττιος (4) (PA 1669)
adoptee: Ἀρίσταρχος (5-6) (PA 1670)
natural father of adoptee: Κυρωνίδης Ξεναινέτου Ἀχαρνεύς (6) (PA 8950)
relationship by blood between adopter and adoptee: by blood, the adopter was the paternal grandfather of the adoptee, but *de jure* the brother of the adoptee's maternal grandfather. (5-6)
Was the adoption challenged? yes, by the son of the adopter's daughter, but only after the death of the adoptee (18sqq.)
Procedure: probably διαδικασία
Date: The adoptee died sometime between 378-371, and the adoption must have taken place before his death (cf. cat.no.10).

cat.no.21 ref.Isaios VI.36sq.,44sq.
type of adoption: posthumous (36)
adopter: Ἐργαμένης Εὐκτήμονος Κηφισιεύς (44) (PA 5047)
adoptee: ?
natural father of adoptee: according to the speaker of Isaios VI, the adoptee was of slave-descent, but Euktemon, the father of the adopter, had accepted him formally as his son and had had him (or his brother, cat. no. 22) enrolled in his phratry (21-26)
relationship by blood between adopter and adoptee: according to the speaker of Isaios VI they were not related at all, according to his opponent they were paternal half-brothers.
Was the adoption challenged? yes, but the speaker does not tell us by whom (37)
Procedure: the adoption was denounced as a fraud in a μίσθωσις οἴκου-procedure in which the adoptee was registered as the orphaned son of the adopter (36), and the judges refused to proceed in leasing the orphan's property (36 and 45).
Date: This attempted adoption must be dated after the death of Philoktemon between 378 and 373(Wyse, p.484, cf. cat. no. 22) and before the law-suit in which Isaios VI was delivered (365/4 or 364/3, Wyse (1904) p.484).

cat.no.22 ref.Isaios VI.36sq.,44sq.
type of adoption: posthumous (36)
adopter: Φιλοκτήμων Εὐκτήμονος Κηφισιεύς (44) (PA 14641)
adoptee: ?
natural father of adoptee: according to the speaker of Isaios VI, the adoptee was of slave-descent, but Euktemon, the father of the adopter, had accepted him formally as his son and had had him (or his brother, cat. no. 21) enrolled in his phratry (21-26)
relationship by blood between adopter and adoptee: according to the speaker of Isaios VI they were not related at all, according to his opponent they were paternal half-brothers.
Was the adoption challenged? yes, but the speaker does not tell us by whom (37)
Procedure: the adoption was denounced as a fraud in a μίσθωσις οἴκου-procedure in which the adoptee was registered as the orphaned son of the adopter (36), and the judges refused to proceed in leasing the orphan's property (36 and 45).
Date: This attempted adoption must be dated after the death of Philoktemon between 378 and 373 (Wyse (1904) p.484) and before the law-suit in which Isaios VI was delivered (365/4 or 364/3, Wyse (1904) p.484).

cat.no.23　　　　　　　　　　　　　　　　　　　　　ref.Isaios XI.49sq.
type of adoption: posthumous (Isaios XI.49)　　　　　　　　[Dem.] XLIII *pass*.
adopter: Μακάρτατος 'Απολήξιδος Προσπάλτιος ([Dem.] XLIII.48,77) (PA 9660)
adoptee: Μακάρτατος (Isaios XI.49, [Dem.] XLIII.77) (PA 9659)
natural father of adoptee: Θεόπομπος Χαριδήμου ἐξ Οἴου ([Dem.] XLIII.22) (PA 7036)
relationship by blood between adopter and adoptee: the adopter was the maternal
　　　　　　　　　　　　　　　　　　　　　　　　　　　　　　uncle of the adoptee
Was the adoption challenged? Lysias frg. LXXXVI, περὶ ἡμικληρίου τῶν Μακαρτάτου χρημάτων is connected with the inheritance left by Makartatos I. It cannot be determined, however, whether the dispute occurred before or after the posthumous adoption had been carried out. Nor is there any information regarding the procedure employed by the rival claimants.
Date: before 360, the earliest possible date of Isaios XI (Wyse (1904) p.677)

cat.no.24　　　　　　　　　　　　　　　　　　　　　ref. [Dem.] XLIII *pass*.
type of adoption: posthumous (11)
adopter: Εὐβουλίδης Φιλάγρου ἐξ Οἴου (24) (PA 5335)
adoptee: Εὐβουλίδης (34-74) (PA 5334)
natural father of adoptee: Σωσίθεος Σωσίου (36sq.,46,74) (PA 13224)
relationship by blood between adopter and adoptee: the adopter was the maternal grandfather of the adoptee (12-13)
Was the adoption challenged? no
Date: ca. 345 (see Humphreys (1983a) p.221, and Thompson (1976) p.63

c2) Replacement of adoptee by posthumous adoption

cat.no.25　　　　　　　　　　　　　　　　　　　　　ref. [Dem.] XLIV.20sq.
type of adoption: posthumous　　　　　　　　　　　　　　cf. cat.nos. 1 and 18
adopter: 'Αρχιάδης Εὐθυμάχου 'Οτρυνεύς (9) (PA 2441)
adoptee: Λεώστρατος (PA 9154)
natural father of adoptee: Λεωκράτους 'Αρχιάδου 'Οτρυνεύς (cf. cat.no.1)
relationship by blood between adopter and adoptee: Leostratos was the grandson of
　　　　　　　　　　　　　　　　　　　　　　　　Archiades' sister's daughter (17, 21)
Was the adoption challenged? no.
Date: ?

cat.no.26　　　　　　　　　　　　　　　　　　　　　ref. [Dem.]XLIV.22 *pass*.
type of adoption: posthumous　　　　　　　　　　　　cf. cat.nos. 1, 18, and 25
adopter: 'Αρχιάδης Εὐθυμάχου 'Οτρυνεύς (9) (PA 2441)
adoptee: Λεωκράτης (PA 9154)
natural father of adoptee: Λεώστρατος 'Αρχιάδου 'Οτρυνεύς (cf. cat.no.25)
relationship by blood between adopter and adoptee: Leokrates was the great-
　　　　　　　　　　　　　　　　　　　　　　grandson of Archiades' sister's daughter (17, 22)
Was the adoption challenged? no.
Date: ?

cat.no.27　　　　　　　　　　　　　　　　　　　　　ref. [Dem.] XLIII.77sq.
type of adoption: posthumous
adopter: Μακάρτατος 'Απολήξιδος Προσπάλτιος ([Dem.] XLIII.48) (PA 9660)
adoptee: ?
natural father of adoptee: Μακάρτατος Μακαρτάτου Προσπάλτιος (PA 9659)
relationship by blood between adopter and adoptee: the adoptee was the grandson of
　　　　　　　　　　　　　　　　　　　　　　　　　　　Makartatos A.P.'s sister.
Was the adoption challenged? no.
Date: prior to ca. 345 (see Humphreys (1983a) p.221, and Thompson (1976) p.63) and after 360.([Dem.]XLIII.31).

d) Adoptions of unknown type

cat.no.28   ref. Plut.*Them*.32
type of adoption: ?
adopter: Λύσανδρος 'Αλωπεκῆθεν (PA 9283)
adoptee: Διοκλῆς (PA 4064)
natural father of adoptee: Θεμιστοκλῆς Νεοκλέους Φρεάρριος (PA 6669)
relationship by blood between adopter and adoptee: Lysandros was Diokles' maternal grandfather.
Was the adoption challenged? ?
Date: probably no later than the close of the V. cent.: the adoptee must have been born prior to 459, the year of Themistokles' death.

cat.no.29   ref. Dio. Hal. *De Din*.12
type of adoption: ?
adopter: 'Αρχεφῶν (PA 2436)
adoptee: Θεόδωρος (PA 6839)
natural father of adoptee: ?
relationship by blood between adopter and adoptee: ?
Was the adoption challenged? Probably: we have the titles of two speeches that appear to have been delivered in this connection.
Date: ?

cat.no.30   ref. Isaios X.4,7,8.
type of adoption: ?
adopter: Ξεναίνετος 'Αχαρνεύς (7,8) (PA 11175)
adoptee: Κυρωνίδης (4,7,8) (PA 8950)
natural father of adoptee: 'Αρίσταρχος Συπαλήττιος (4) (PA 1669)
relationship by blood between adopter and adoptee: Xenainetos was the maternal grandfather of Kyronides (4).
Was the adoption challenged? no.
Date:? (possibly long before 378-1, the date of Isaios X (Wyse (1904) p.652).

cat.no.31   ref. Isaios IX.2,33.
type of adoption: ?
adopter: ?
adoptee: Θούδιππος 'Αραφήνιος (PA 7252)
natural father of adoptee: ?
relationship by blood between adopter and adoptee: ?
Was the adoption challenged? ?
Date: before 369, the year of Astyphilos' death (cf. cat. no. 14).

cat.no.32   ref. Isaios VII.23.
type of adoption: ?
adopter: 'Ιππολοχίδης Θρασυμέδου Λουσιεύς (PA 7643, Davies, *APF*, p.46).
adoptee: Θρασύβουλος (18) (PA 7603)
natural father of adoptee: Αἰσχίνης Λουσιεύς (18) (PA 358)
relationship by blood between adopter and adoptee: ?
Was the adoption challenged? ?
Date: before 357/6, the terminus post quem of Isaios VII (cf. cat. no.4)

cat.no.33   ref. [Dem.] XLIII.37,45
type of adoption: ?
adopter: Ἀρχίμαχος (37) (PA 2515)
adoptee: ?
natural father of adoptee: ?
relationship by blood between adopter and adoptee: Archimachos was the grandfather of the adoptee (37).
Was the adoption challenged? ?
Date: prior to ca. 345, the date of [Dem.] XLIII (cf. cat. no.24)

cat.no.34   ref. [Dem.] LVIII.30-32
type of adoption: ?
adopter: Αἰσχύλος Ἀ[θμον]εύς or Α[ἰξων]εύς (Davies, *APF*, p.6, no.436)
adoptee: Χαρίδημος (PA 15374)
natural father of adoptee: Ἰσχόμαχος (PA 7729)
relationship by blood between adopter and adoptee: ?
Was the adoption challenged? no.
Date: Hansen (1974) dates [Dem.] LVIII to shortly before 340 (p.35, cat. no.23).

cat.no.35   ref. [Dem.] XLII.21sq., 27.
type of adoption: ?
adopter: Φιλόστρατος Διονυσίου Κολωνῆθεν ([Dem.] XLII.21 and LIX.23) (PA 14734)
adoptee: Φαίνιππος ([Dem.] XLII.21) (PA 13978)
natural father of adoptee: Κάλλιππος ([Dem.] XLII.21) (PA 8058)
relationship by blood between adopter and adoptee: Philostratos was the maternal grandfather of Phainippos ([Dem.] XLII.27)
Was the adoption challenged? ?
Date: [Dem.] XLII is dated to after 330/29 by Blass (1898) III, pp.505sq.). Philostratos was still alive when [Dem.] LIX was delivered ca.340.

cat.no.36   ref. Plut. *Mor.* 843A
type of adoption: ?
adopter: Λυκόφρων Λυκούργου Βουτάδης (PA 9261)
adoptee: Λυκόφρων (PA 9262)
natural father of adoptee: Κλεόμβροτος Δεινοκράτους Ἀχαρνεύς (PA 9262)
relationship by blood between adopter and adoptee: Lykophron L.B. was the maternal grandfather of the adoptee.
Was the adoption challenged? ?
Date: ? (III cent.? The adoptee was the great-grandson (SDS) of Lykourgos who died ca.325).

Stemmata

These stemmata are not meant to be detailed genealogical tables; rather, they are intended as a guide to the reader who may find it difficult to remember who is who in each particular case of adoption. For that reason I have tried to keep the stemmata as simple as possible: they only show the family-relationship between adopter and adoptee, and, if the adoption was attacked, between the adopter and the opponents of the adoptee. The tables only show the relationships as they were represented in court: I have not tried to find out the truth behind the claims of a given speaker. However, relationships that were contested have been marked with dotted lines, and I have indicated if a marrriage was disputed by adding a question mark to the ≈. The names of adopters and adoptees have been written in bold and italics, those of the adoptees' opponents in bold. M=Male, F=Female.

Cat. no.1, 18, 25, 26

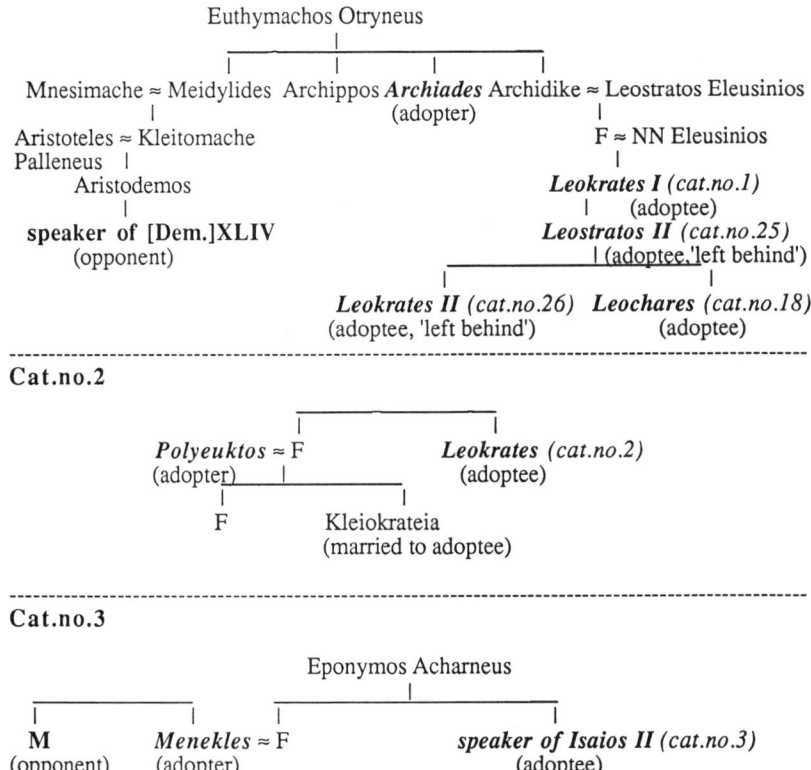

Cat.no.2

Cat.no.3

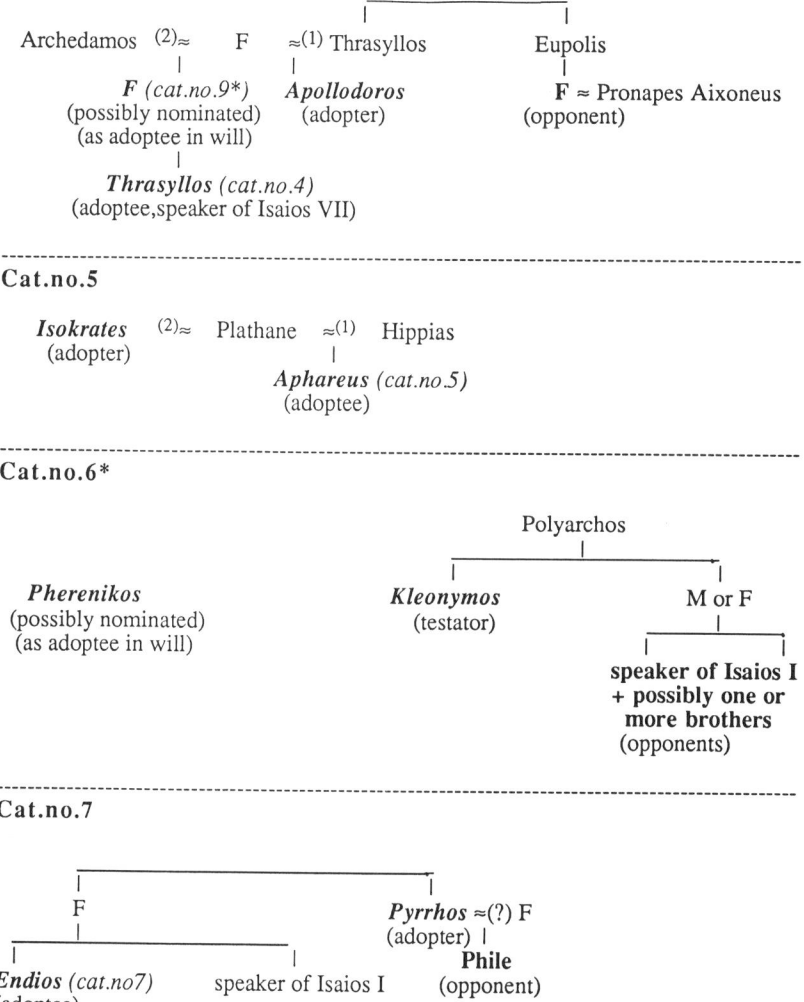

Cat.no.8

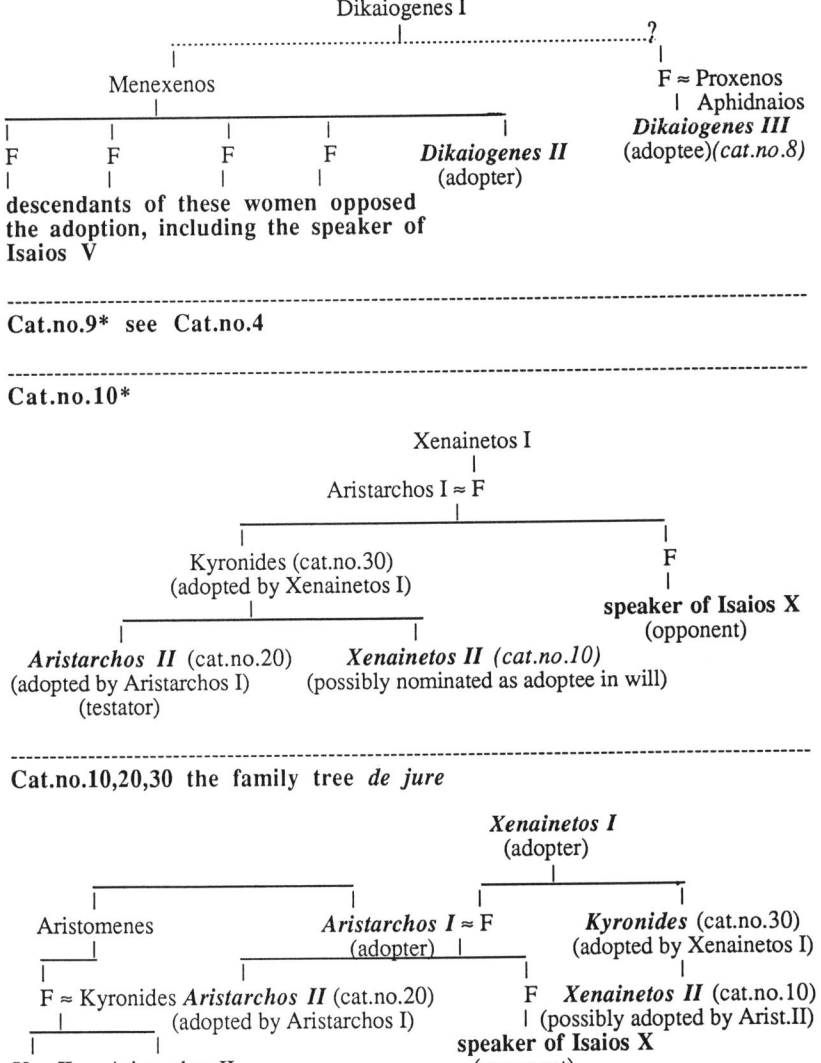

Cat.no.9* see Cat.no.4

Cat.no.10*

Cat.no.10,20,30 the family tree *de jure*

Cat.no.11,12*

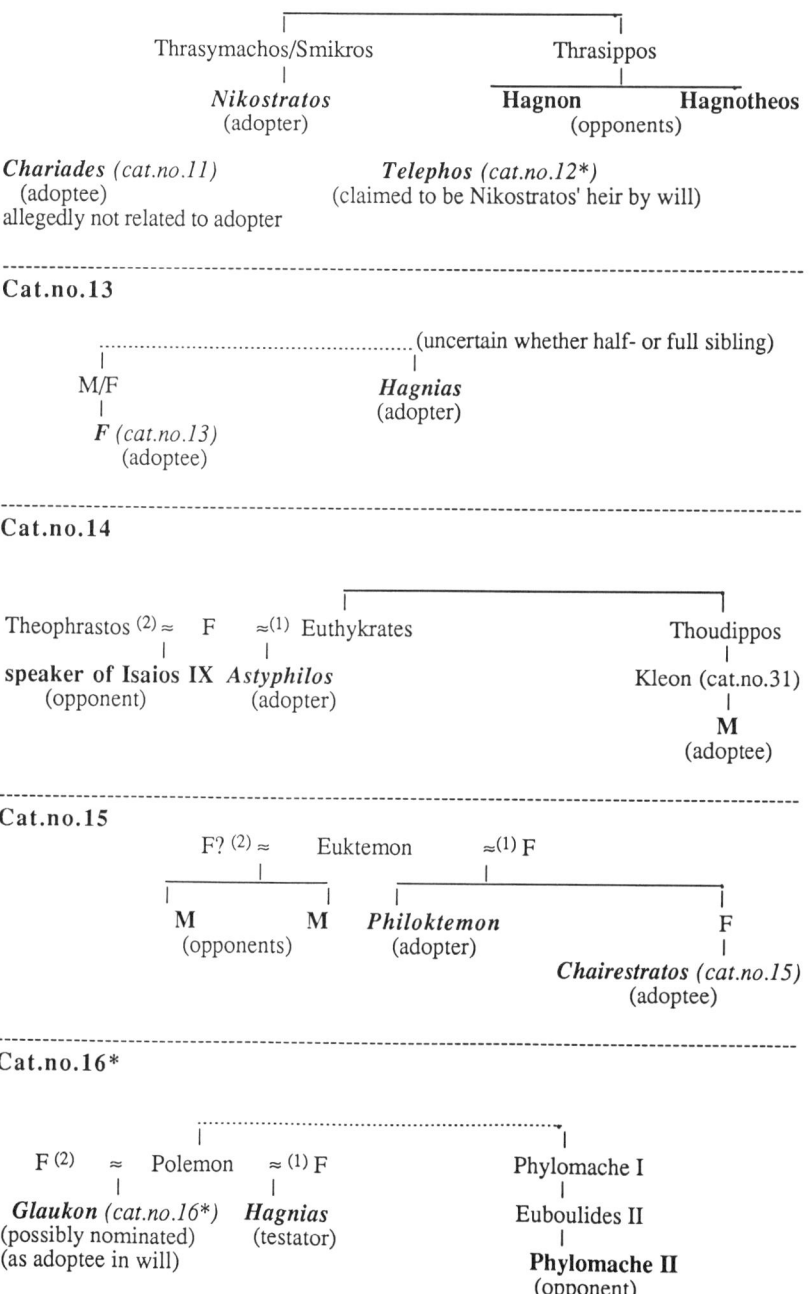

Cat.no.13

Cat.no.14

Cat.no.15

Cat.no.16*

Cat.no.17

```
                    |————————————————————————|
                Theophon                    F ≈ Stratokles
                (adopter)                        |
                              |————————|————|————|————|
                          F (cat.no.17)  F    F    F    M
                           (adoptee)
```

Cat.no.18 see cat.no.1

Cat.no.19

```
    M      (2) ≈      F      ≈ (1) M
(adopter)___|                   |
   |    |    |              Diokles (cat.no.19)
   F    F    F               (adoptee)
(opponents)
```

Cat.no.20

```
                        |——————————————|
                             Xenainetos I
                        |              |
                   Aristomenes    Aristarchos I ≈ F
                        |          (adopter)    |
                   |————|————————————————|            |
                   M    F ≈ Kyronides (cat.no.30)     F
                        (adopted by Xenainetos I)     |
                        |——————————————|       speaker of Isaios X
                        |              |          (opponent)
              Aristarchos II (cat.no.20)  Xenainetos II (cat.no.10)
              (adopted by Aristarchos I)
```

Cat.no.10,20,30 the family tree *de jure*

```
                                    Xenainetos I
                                     (adopter)
                                         |
              |——————————————————|————————————————|
          Aristomenes       Aristarchos I ≈ F    Kyronides (cat.no.30)
              |               (adopter)  |       (adopted by Xenainetos I)
              |——————————|———————————|          |
         F ≈ Kyronides  Aristarchos II (cat.no.20)   F   Xenainetos II (cat.no.10)
              |         (adopted by Aristarchos I)   |   (possibly adopted by Arist.II)
         |————|                                 speaker of Isaios X
         Xen.II  Aristarchos II                    (opponent)
```

Cat.no.21

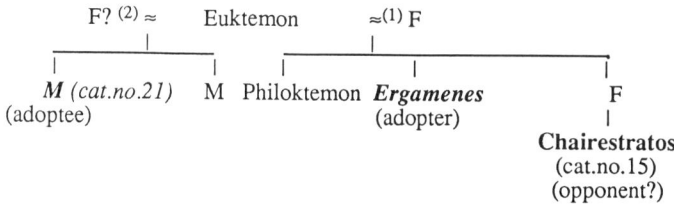

Cat.no.22

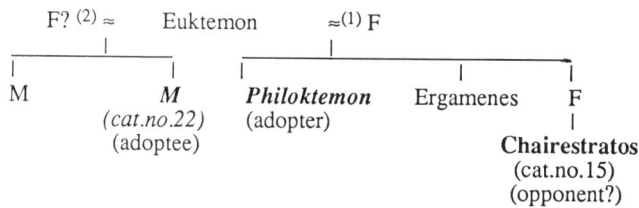

Cat.no.23, 27

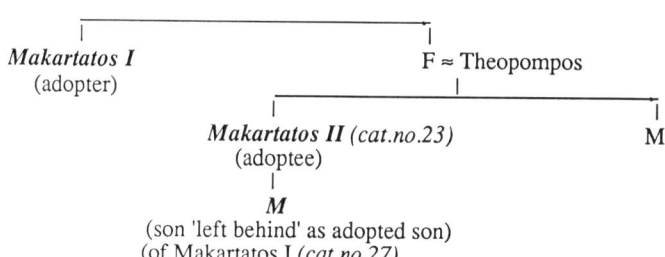

Cat.no.24

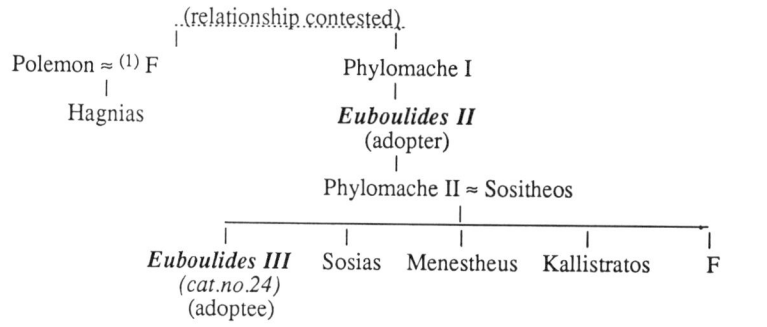

Cat.no.25 see cat.no.1

Cat.no.26 see cat.no.1

Cat.no.27 see cat.no.23

Cat.no.28

```
                    Lysandros
                    (adopter)
                        |
              Archippe ≈ Themistokles
                        |
    ┌────┬────┬────┬────┬────┬────┬────┬────┐
 Diokles  M    M    M    M    F    F    F    F
(cat.no.28)
 (adoptee)
```

Cat.no.29

Theodoros adopted by Archephon. Nothing is known about the relationship between adopter and adoptee, nor do we know who attacked the adoption in court.

Cat.no.30

```
                         Xenainetos I
                          (adopter)
                              |
                   Aristarchos I ≈ F
                              |
            ┌─────────────────┼─────────────────┐
       Kyronides (cat.no.30)  M                  F
         (adoptee)
```

Cat.no.31

Thoudippos Araphenios adopted by NN. Nothing is known about the relationship between adopter and adoptee.

Cat.no.32

Thrasyboulos adopted by Hippolochides Thrasymedou Lousieus. Nothing is known about the relationship between adopter and adoptee.

Cat.no.33

```
          Archimachos
           (adopter)
               |
               F
               |
          M (cat.no.33)
```

Cat.no.34

Charidemos Ischomachou adopted by Aischylos Athmoneus or Aixoneus. Nothing is known about the relationship between adopter and adoptee.

Cat.no.35

Philostratos Dionysiou Kolonethen
(adopter)
|
F
|
Phainippos Kalippou (cat.no.35)

Cat.no.36

Lykophron Lykourgou Boutades
(adopter)
|
Kallisto
|
Lykophron Kleombrotou Acharneus (cat.no.36)
(adoptee)

Bibliography

Adeleye, G. (1983): "The purpose of the dokimasia" in *Greek, Roman, and Byzantine Studies* XXIV, pp. 295-306.
Andrewes, A. (1961): "Philochoros on phratries" in *Journal of Hellenic Studies* LXXXI, pp.1-15.
Asheri, D. (1960): "L'οἶκος ἔρημος nel diritto successorio attico" in *Archivio Guiridico* (6ᵉ ser.) XXVIII, pp.7-24.
Asheri, D. (1963): "Laws of inheritance, distribution of land, and political constitutions" in *Historia* XII, pp.1-21.
Baiter,G and H.Sauppe (1850), *Oratores Attici* I-II, Zürich
Beauchet, L. (1897): *Histoire du droit privé de la république athénienne* (vols. I-IV), Paris (repr. Amsterdam 1969).
Becker, W.G. (1932): *Platons Gesetze und das griechische Familienrecht*, (Münchener Beiträge zur Papyrusforschung und antiken Rechtsgeschichte 14) München.
Biscardi, A. (1983): "Osservazioni critiche sulla terminologia διαθήκη - διατίθεσθαι" in *Symposion 1979*, pp. 23-35.
Blass, F.(1898), *Die attische Beredsamkeit* I-III, Leipzig
Boncompto, F.S. (1954): "ἐπισκήπτειν como acto de ultimo voluntad" in *Revue internationale des droits de l'antiquité* I, pp.259-268.
Bourriot, F. (1976):*Recherches sur la nature du Génos. Étude d'histoire sociale athénienne* (vols. I-II), Diss. Lille, Paris.
Brindesi, F. (1961):*La famiglia attica. Il matrimonio e l'adozione.* Firenze.
Broadbent, M. (1968):*Studies in Greek Genealogy*, Leiden.
Brown, P.G.McC. (1983): "Menander's dramatic technique and the law of Athens" in*Classical Quarterly* XXXIII, pp.412-420.
Bruck, E.F. (1909): *Die Schenkung auf den Todesfall im griechischen und römischen Recht, zugleich ein Beitrag zur Geschichte des Testaments*, (Studien zur Erläuterung des bürgerlichen Recht 31), Breslau.
Bruck, E.F. (1926):*Totenteil und Seelgerät im griechischen Recht*, (Münchener Beiträge zur Papyrusforschung und antiken Rechtsgeschichte 9) München.
Caillemer, E. (1879): *Le droit de succession légitime à Athènes*, Paris.
Cartledge, P.A and F.D. Harvey (1985) [eds.]:*Crux: Essays in Greek History presented to G.E.M. de Ste. Croix on his 75th Birthday*, Exeter & London.
Cartledge, P.A., P.Millett, and S.Todd (1990) [eds.]:*Nomos: Essays in Athenian Law, Politics and Society*, Cambridge.

Cox, C.A. (1988): "Sibling relationships in classical Athens: brother-sister ties" in *Journal of Family History* XIII, pp.377-396.
Cox, C.A. (1988b): "Sisters, daughters and the deme of marriage: a note" in *Journal of Hellenic Studies* CVIII, pp.185-188.
Davies, J.K. (1971):*Athenian Propertied Families*, Oxford.
Davies, J.K. (1977): "Athenian citizenship: the descent-group and the alternatives" in *Classical Journal* LXXIII (1977-78), pp.105-121.
Dover, K.J. (1974): *Greek Popular Morality in the Time of Plato and Aristotle*, Oxford.
Erdmann, W. (1934):*Die Ehe im alten Griechenland,* (Münchener Beiträge zur Papyrusforschung und antiken Rechtsgeschichte 20), München.
Falkner and de Luce [eds.] (1989):*Old Age in Greek and Latin Literature*, New York.
Finley, M.I. (1989): "The Elderly in Classical Antiquity" in *Old Age in Greek and Latin Literature* [eds. Falkner and de Luce], pp.1-20, repr. from *Greece and Rome* XXVIII (1981), pp.156-171.
Finley, M.I. (1952):*Studies in Land and Credit in Ancient Athens, 500-200 B.C. The Horos inscriptions*, New Brunswick (repr. with an introduction by P.Millett, 1985).
Foxhall, L. (1989): "Household, gender, and property in Athens" in *Classical Quarterly* XXXIX, pp. 22-43.
French, A. (1991): "Economic conditions in fourth-century Athens" in *Greece and Rome* XXXVIII, pp.24-40.
Gabrielsen, V. (1986): "Φανερὰ and ἀφανὴς οὐσία in classical Athens" in *Classica et Mediaevalia* XXXVII, pp.99-114.
Garland, R. (1985):*The Greek Way of Death,* London.
Gernet, L. (1924): "Sur l'épiclérat" in *Revue des études grecques* XXXIV, pp. 337-379.
Gernet, L. (1938): "Introduction à l'étude du droit grec ancien" in *Archives d'histoire du droit oriental* II, pp.261-292 (repr. in German translation in *ZGR*, pp.4-38)
Gernet, L. (1955): *Droit et société dans la Grèce ancienne*, Paris.
Golden, M. (1979): "Demosthenes and the age of majority at Athens" in *Phoenix* XXXIII, pp. 25-39
Golden, M. (1990):*Children and Childhood in Classical Athens*, Baltimore.
Gomme, A.W. and F.H. Sandbach (1973):*Menander, A Commentary*, Oxford.
Gould, J. (1980): "Law, custom, and myth: aspects of the social position of women in classical Athens" in *Journal of Hellenic Studies* C, pp.38-59.

Hansen, M.H. (1973): *Atimistraffen i Athen i klassisk tid*, Odense.
Hansen, M.H. (1974): *The Sovereignty of the People's Court in Athens in the Fourth Century B.C. and the Action against Unconstitutional Proposals*, Odense.
Hansen, M.H. (1976): *Apagoge, Endeixis, and Ephegesis against Kakourgoi, Atimoi, and Pheugontes*, Odense.
Hansen, M.H. (1981): "Initiative and decision: the separation of powers in fourth-century Athens" in *Greek, Roman, and Byzantine Studies* XXII, pp. 345-370.
Hansen, M.H. (1983): *The Athenian Ecclesia*, Copenhagen.
Hansen, M.H. (1986): *Demography and Democracy*, Herning.
Hansen, M.H. (1991):*The Athenian Democracy in the Age of Demosthenes*, Oxford.
Hanson, V.D. (1989): *The Western Way of War: Infantry Battle in Classical Greece*, New York.
Hardcastle, M. (1980): "Some non legal arguments in Athenian inheritance-cases" in *Prudentia* XII, pp.11-22.
Harrison, A.R.W. (1968-71): *The Law of Athens* (vols. I-II), [I.] *The Family and Property*, Oxford 1968, [II.] *Procedure*, [ed. D.M.MacDowell], Oxford 1971.
Hedrick, C.W. (1990): *The Decrees of the Demotionidai*, American Classical Studies 22, Atlanta, Georgia.
Hedrick, C.W. (1991): "Phratry shrines of Attica and Athens" in *Hesperia* LX, pp.241-268.
Hruza, E. (1892): *Die Ehebegründung nach attischem Rechte*, Erlangen u. Leipzig (repr. 1979 by Arno Press).
Hubbard, T.K.: "Old Men in the Youthful Plays of Aristophanes" in *Old Age in Greek and Latin Literature* [eds. Falkner and de Luce], pp.90-113.
Humphreys, S.C. (1974): "The nothoi of Kynosarges" in *Journal of Hellenic Studies* XCIV, pp. 88-95.
Humphreys, S.C. (1977-78): "Public and private interests in classical Athens" in *Classical Journal* LXXIII, pp. 97-104, repr. in Humphreys (1983b), pp.22-32.
Humphreys, S.C. and A. Momigliano (1980): Foreword to the 1980 edition of N.D. Fustel de Coulanges, *The Ancient City*, Baltimore, repr. in Humphreys (1983b) pp. 131-143.
Humphreys, S.C. (1980b): "Family tombs and tomb cult in ancient Athens" in *Journal of Hellenic Studies* C, pp.96-126, repr. in Humphreys (1983b), pp.79-130.

Humphreys, S.C. (1981): "Death and time" in *Mortality and Immortality* [eds. S.C.Humphreys and H.King], London, pp.261-283, repr. in Humphreys (1983b), pp.144-164.
Humphreys, S.C. (1983a): "The date of Hagnias' death" in *Classical Philology* LXXVIII, pp. 219-225.
Humphreys, S.C. (1983b): *The Family, Women, and Death*, London.
Humphreys, S.C. (1986): "Kinship patterns in Athenian courts" in *Greek, Roman, and Byzantine Studies* XXVII,pp. 57-91.
Hunter, V. (1990): "Gossip and the politics of reputation in classical Athens" in *Phoenix* XLIV, pp. 299-325.
Isager, S. (1982): "The marriage pattern in classical Athens: men and women in Isaeus" in *Classica et Mediaevalia* XXXIII, pp. 81-96.
Jones, J.W. (1956): *The Law and Legal Theory of the Greeks*, Oxford.
Just, R. (1989): *Women in Athenian Law and Life*, London.
Karabelias, E. (1975): "L'épiclérat dans la Comédie Nouvelle et dans les sources Latines" in *Symposion 1971*, pp. 215-255.
Karabelias, E. (1979): "Contribution à l'étude de l'épidikasie attique" in *Symposion 1974*, pp. 201-227.
Karabelias, E. (1989): "La succession *ab intestat* en droit attique" in *Symposion 1982*, pp. 41-63.
Kirchner, J.(1901-3): *Prosopographia Attica*, Berlin.
Kurtz, D. and J. Boardman (1971): *Greek Burial Customs*, Thames and Hudson, London.
Labarbe, J. (1956): "L'âge correspondant au sacrifice du κούρειον et les données historiques du sixième discours d'Isée" in *Bulletin de l'Académie Royale de Belgique* XXXIX, pp. 358-394.
Lacey, W.K. (1968):*The Family in Classical Greece*, Thames and Hudson, London, republished by the author in 1980 (Auckland, New Zealand.)
Lambert, S.D. (1986): *The Ionian Phyle and Phratry in Archaic and Classical Athens. Diss. Oxford.*
Lane Fox, R. (1985): "Aspects of inheritance in the Greek world" in *Crux: Essays in Greek History presented to G.E.M. de Ste. Croix on his 75th Birthday*, [eds. Cartledge and Harvey] Exeter & London, pp. 208-232.
Lewis, N. (1982): "Aphairesis in Athenian law and custom" in *Symposion 1977*, pp. 161-178.
Lipsius, J.H. (1905-15): *Das attische Recht und Rechtsverfahren* (vols. I-III), Leipzig.
MacDowell, D.M. (1976): "Bastards as Athenian citizens" in *Classical Quarterly* XXVI, pp.88-91.
MacDowell, D.M. (1978): *The Law in Classical Athens*, London.
MacDowell, D.M. (1982): "Love versus the law: an essay on Menander's *Aspis* " in *Greece and Rome* XXIX, pp. 42-52.

MacDowell, D.M. (1989): "The *oikos* in Athenian law" in *Classical Quarterly* XXXIX, pp. 1-21.
MacDowell, D.M. (1989b): "The authencity of Demosthenes 29 (against Aphobos III) as a source of information about Athenian law" in *Symposion 1985*, pp.253-262.
Maffi, A. (1989): "Matrimonio, concubinato e filiazione illegittima nell' Atene degli oratori" in *Symposion 1985*, pp.177-214
Miles, J.C. (1950): "The Attic law of intestate succession" in *Hermathena* LXXV, pp.69-77 (repr. in German translation in *Zur Griechischen Rechtsgeschichte* [ed. Berneker], Darmstadt 1968, pp. 655-665).
Millett, P. (1991): *Lending and Borrowing in Ancient Athens*, Cambridge.
Mossé, C. (1989a): "Quelques remarques sur la famille à Athènes à la fin du IVème siècle: Le témoignage du théatre de Ménandre" in *Symposion 1982*, pp. 129-134
Mossé, C. (1989b): "Le contre Spoudias de Démosthènes et les droits économiques des femmes d'Athènes au IVème siècle" in *Symposion 1985*, pp. 215-219.
Nielsen, Th. Heine et al. (1989): "Athenian grave monuments and social class" in *Greek, Roman, and Byzantine Studies* XXX, pp. 411-420.
Osborne, M. (1981-83): *Naturalization in Athens I-IV. Testimonia; The Law and Practice*, Bruxelles.
Osborne, R. (1985): *Demos: The Discovery of Classical Attica*, Cambridge.
Paoli, U.E. (1946): "La legittima afèresi dell'ἐπίκληρος" in *Miscellanea Giovanni Mercati* V, Roma, pp.524-538 (repr. in *Altri studi di diritto greco e romano*, Milano 1976, pp.363-376).
Paoli, U.E. (1961): "Note giuridiche sul Δύσκολος di Menandro" in *Museum Helveticum* XVIII (1961) pp.53sqq. (reprinted in *Altri studi di diritto greco e romano*, Milano 1976, pp.559-571).
Patterson, C.B. (1981): *Pericles' Citizenship Law of 451/0 B.C.*, New York, repr. 1988 by Ayer Company.
Patterson, C.B. (1990): "Those Athenian bastards" in *Classical Antiquity* IX, pp.40-73
Podo, M. (1957): *L'adozione sul diritto attico*, Roma (*not accessible*).
Polácek, V. (1967): "Quelques remarques sur l'adoption dans le «Dyskolos» de Menandre" in *Revue internationale des droits de l'antiquité* XIV, pp.157-167.
Rhodes, P.J. (1978): "Bastards as Athenian citizens" in *Classical Quarterly* XXVII, pp. 89-92.
Richardson, B.E. (1933): *Old Age among the Ancient Greeks*, Baltimore.

Rosivach, V.J. (1984): "Aphairesis and apoleipsis: a study of the sources" in *Revue internationale des droits de l'antiquité* XXXI, pp.193-230.
Rubinstein, L.et al. (1991): "Adoption in Hellenistic and Roman Athens" in *Classica et Mediaevalia* XLII, pp.139-151.
Ruschenbusch, E. (1957): "δικαστήριον πάντων κύριον" in *Historia* VI, pp. 257-274 (repr. in *Zur Griechischen Rechtsgeschichte* [ed. Berneker] Darmstadt 1968, pp. 350-374).
Ruschenbusch, E. (1962): "διατίθεσθαι τὰ ἑαυτοῦ. Ein Beitrag zum sogenannten Testamentgesetz des Solon" in *Zeitschrift der Savigny-Stiftung für Rechtsgeschichte, rom. Abt.* LXXIX, pp. 307-311.
Ruschenbusch, E. (1987): "Demosthenes' erste freiwillige Trierarchie und die Datierung des Euböa-Unternehmens vom Jahre 357" in *ZPE* LXVII, pp.158sq.
Sainte Croix, G.E.M. de (1970): "Athenian family law" (review of Harrison:1968) in *Classical Review* XX, pp. 387-390.
Schaps, D.: "Women in Greek inheritance law" in *Classical Quarterly* XXV, pp.53-57.
Schaps, D. (1977): "The woman least mentioned: etiquette and women's names" in *Classical Quarterly* XXVII, pp.323-330.
Schaps, D. (1979): *Economic Rights of Women in Ancient Greece*, Edinburgh.
Sealey, R. (1987): *The Athenian Republic. Democracy or the Rule of Law?* University Park.
Sealey, R. (1990): *Women and Law in Classical Greece*, Chapel Hill.
Sissa, G. (1986): "La famille dans la cité grecque (V-IV siècle avant J.-C.)" in *Histoire de la famille* [eds. A. Burguière *et al.*] Paris, pp.163-193.
Symposion 1971: Vorträge zur griechischen und hellenistischen Rechtsgeschichte [ed. H.J.Wolff], Köln & Wien 1975.
Symposion 1974: Vorträge zur griechischen und hellenistischen Rechtsgeschichte [ed. Biscardi], Köln & Wien 1979.
Symposion 1977: Vorträge zur griechischen und hellenistischen Rechtsgeschichte [eds. Modrzejewski and Liebs], Köln & Wien 1982.
Symposion 1979: Vorträge zur griechischen und hellenistischen Rechtsgeschichte [ed. Dimakis], Köln & Wien 1983.
Symposion 1982. Vorträge zur griechischen und hellenistischen Rechtsgeschichte [ed. Nieto], Köln & Wien 1989.
Symposion 1985. Vorträge zur griechischen und hellenistischen Rechtsgeschichte [ed. Thür], Köln & Wien 1989.
Thompson, W.E. (1968): "An Interpretation of the 'Demotionid' Decrees" in *Symbolae Osloenses* XLII, pp. 51-69
Thompson, W.E. (1976): *De Hagniae Hereditate*, Leiden.

Thompson, W.E. (1981): "Athenian attitudes towards wills" in *Prudentia* XIII, pp.13-25.
Todd, S. and P.Millett (1990): "Law, society and Athens" in *Nomos: Essays in Athenian Law, Politics and Society* [eds. P.Cartledge *et al.*], Cambridge, pp. 1-18.
Traill, J.S. (1975): *The Political Organization of Attica*, Princeton, N.J.
Walters, J.S. (1983): "Pericles' citizenship law" in *Classical Antiquity* N.S.II.2, pp. 314-336.
Wankel, H. (1988):"Demosthenes' erste freiwillige Trierarchie und die Datierung des Euböa-Unternehmens vom Jahre 357" in *ZPE* LXXI, pp.199sq.
Whitehead, D. (1986): *The Demes of Attica, 508/7 - ca. 250 B.C.*, Princeton, N.J.
Wevers, R.F. (1969): *Isaeus: Chronology, Prosopography, and Social History*, The Hague.
Wolff, H.J. (1946): "The Origin of Judicial Litigation among the Greeks" in *Traditio* IV, pp. 31-87.
Wolff, H.J. (1957): "Die Grundlagen des griechischen Vertragsrechts" in *Zeitschrift der Savigny-Stiftung für Rechtsgeschichte, rom. Abt.* LXXIV, pp.26-72.
Wolff, H.J. (1978): "Polis und Civitas" in *Zeitschrift der Savigny-Stiftung für Rechtsgeschichte, rom. Abt.* XCVI, pp.1-14.
Wyse, W. (1904): *The Speeches of Isaeus*, Cambridge.
Zur griechischen Rechtsgeschichte (ZGR) [ed. Berneker], Darmstadt 1968.

When referring to the speeches of Isaios I have relied almost exclusively on Wyse's edition (1904), and on the Oxford edition when quoting Demosthenes. All translations of the Greek into English are my own, except otherwise stated.

Index of Sources

AISCHINES
Against Timarchos
I.13   70n.24
I.13-4   66n.6
I.28   66n.7
I.102-4   64
I.114   44n.43

Against Ktesiphon
III.21   18,20n.14
III.77   70n.26

ANDOKIDES
On the mysteries
I.74   64n.3
I.126-7   49n.58

[Against Alkibiades]
IV.15   86n.58

ANTIPHON
On the murder of Herodes
V.8   12n.30

Frg.IV   58n.78

ARISTOPHANES
Frogs
417   49n.58

Wasps
583-86   97

ARISTOTLE
[Atheniaion Politeia]
35.2   62,80,86n.59
42.1   18,38
43.4   39
55.3   66n.7,75
62.1   44n.43

[Problemata]
950B   75n.40,114

DEINARCHOS
Against Aristogeiton
II.8   70n.27

DEMOSTHENES
Third Olynthiac
III.4   23n.38

Against Leptines
XX.102   86n.59

Against Timokrates
XXIV.60   64n.3
XXIV.103-7   64n.3
XXIV.107   70n.24

Against Aphobos I
XXVII.13   47n.52
XXVII.13-6   83n.53

Against Aphobos II
XXVIII.1-7   101
XXVIII.5   47n.52
XXVIII.6   83n.53
XXVIII.15-6 83n.53

For Phormion
XXXVI   83

Against Nausimachos and Xenopeithes
XXXVIII.17   50n.62

Against Spoudias
XLI   56,96
XLI.3   30
XLI.3-5   55,95,117
XLI.7-9   30
XLI.9   21n.20
XLI.10   85
XLI.20   21n.20
XLI.27   30

[Against Phainippos]
XLII.21   98n.16
XLII.21-2   125
XLII.27   125

[Against Makartatos]
XLIII   4,39n.16,41,52,73,76,
             89,106,123
XLIII.3-4   120
XLIII.4   120
XLIII.5   39,40n.26
XLIII.11   123
XLIII.11-3   69n.22,112n.7
XLIII.11-5   42n.33
XLIII.12-3   123
XLIII.13   44n.39
XLIII.14   36
XLIII.15   42n.31,48n.55,
             52.69,53
XLIII.16   50n.62,108
XLIII.20   25n.48
XLIII.22   123
XLIII.23   120
XLIII.24   123

XLIII.29	120	XLIV.43	74n.39,109n.6
XLIII.31	120,123	XLIV.44	58n.79,59n.86
XLIII.34	123	XLIV.45	25n.45,43n.35,50n.63, 121
XLIII.36-7	123		
XLIII.37	98n.16,125	XLIV.46	51n.64,58n.79,117
XLIII.42	121	XLIV.47-8	59n.86
XLIII.45	125	XLIV.48-51	51n.64
XLIII.46	123	XLIV.49	51n.66
XLIII.48	123	XLIV.51	51n.66
XLIII.51	2n.3,42n.32	XLIV.52	58n.79
XLIII.55	25n.48	XLIV.53-6	40n.22
XLIII.58	71	XLIV.57-9	50n.63
XLIII.74	123	XLIV.61	28n.63
XLIII.75	105n.1,106	XLIV.63	59n.83,76
XLIII.76	106	XLIV.63-4	59n.86
XLIII.77	58,109,123	XLIV.64	58n.78
XLIII.77-8	58n.81,69n.21,123	XLIV.66	28n.64,44n.41,74n.39, 109n.6
XLIII.78	58,108		
XLIII.78-80	69n.22	XLIV.68	17,18,58n.78,59n.83, 59n.86
XLIII.81-2	42n.33		
XLIII.82	37		

Against Stephanos I

XLV	83
XLV.70	64

[Against Leochares]

XLIV	4,26,27,39n.16,51,58, 60,73,121
XLIV.6	51n.66
XLIV.9	30n.67,117,121,123
XLIV.10	30n.67
XLIV.17	22n.29,117,121,123
XLIV.18	21n.23
XLIV.19	40n.25,117
XLIV.19-22	121
XLIV.20-2	123
XLIV.21	123
XLIV.21-2	26n.56,58n.79,121
XLIV.22	123
XLIV.23	59
XLIV.24	59n.86
XLIV.26	43n.37,58n.79
XLIV.28	58n.79
XLIV.29	40n.22,51n.64,121
XLIV.32	72
XLIV.32-4	51n.65,69n.22
XLIV.33-4	28n.63
XLIV.34	43n.35,58n.79
XLIV.35	58n.79
XLIV.35-40	26n.57,38,48n.54
XLIV.35-41	44n.42
XLIV.36	44n.41
XLIV.37-42	44n.43
XLIV.38	43n.37
XLIV.39	58n.79
XLIV.40	43n.37,44n.41,59n84
XLIV.41	59n.85,121
XLIV.42	121
XLIV.41-2	27n.58
XLIV.42-3	40n.22,51n.64
XLIV.43	28n.64,43n.37,44n.41,

[Against Stephanos II]

XLVI	83,84
XLVI.14	10n.24,11,16
XLVI.15	18,83
XLVI.20	90
XLVI.22	107n.2
XLVI.23	40n.26,46n.48
XLVI.24	57,84n.54
XLVI.28	34n.5,67n.14

[Against Olympiodoros]

XLVIII	73,108
XLVIII.12	69n.22,70n.26,71n.32

[Against Dionysodoros]

LVI.2	35n.7

Against Euboulides

LVII.8-14	44n.43
LVII.54	49n.58
LVII.70	66n.7

[Against Theokrines]

LVIII.30-1	39n.15
LVIII.30-2	45n.45,60,125
LVIII.31	60n.89

[Against Neaira]

LIX.23	125
LIX.48	5n.9
LIX.60	37
LIX.64-7	5n.9

DIOGENES LAERTIOS
Platon
41-3   86
DIONYSIOS OF HALIKARNASSOS
Deinarchos
12   124

Isaios
15   40n.26,86n.60

Isokrates
18   118

HELLENICA OXYRHYNCHIA
7.1   41n.29

HYPEREIDES
Frg.LXIII 90n.3
(B.Teubn.)

INSCRIPTIONS
Arch.Eph.(1918)
pp.73-100   42n.30
IG II^2 417   30n.66,60n.90
IG II^2 1237   36
IG II^2 1623   30n.68
IG II^2 1742   120
IG II^2 2930   11n.29
IG II^2 3520   20n.15
IG II^2 3909   20n.15
IG II^2 4720   20n.15
IG II^2 4721   20n.15
IG II^2 4722   20n.15
IG II^2 6482   20n.15
IG II^2 9735   11n.29,20n.15
IG II^2 9949   20n.15
IG XII.593 70n.28

ISAIOS
On the estate of Kleonymos
I   4,39n.15,67,80,118
I.4   118
I.6   118
I.10   69n.22,73,76
I.11   62n.1
I.14   23n.35
I.20-1   62n.1
I.25   57
I.31   118
I.39-40   64
I.43   62n.1,76
I.47   65n.4

On the estate of Menekles
II   4,17,29,31,39n.16,62,

II (ctd.)   71,74,76,117
II.1   17n.3,62n.1
II.2   40n.23,117
II.3   117
II.3-4   21n.22
II.5-10   117
II.6   22n.30
II.7   21n.24
II.10   63,68n.16,110
II.11   21n.22
II.12   34
II.12-4   33
II.13   17n.2,66n.10
II.14   53n.71,117
II.14-5   62n.1
II.15   67n.12
II.17   40n.23,117
II.19   17n.3
II.21-3   22n.27
II.24   6n.11,117
II.25   17n.3,62n.1
II.29   30n.70
II.35   30
II.35-7   68n.16
II.36-7   69n.22,70
II.38   17n.3,62n.1
II.42   30n.71
II.45   67n.12
II.45-7   69n.22
II.46-47   70

On the estate of Pyrrhos
III   4,39n.15,73,78,79,91,
            118
III.1   91n.4,118
III.2   30
III.2-3   78n.43
III.3   91n.5
III.3-6   79n.45
III.6   23n.36
III.8   30
III.8-14   5n.9
III.13-8   79n.45
III.18   30
III.25   30
III.41-3   95n.11
III.48   17n.5
III.50   90n.3
III.58   50n.62
III.60   40n.26
III.61   81
III.64   94,98
III.68   95
III.68-9   17n.5
III.72-3   91
III.73   35,92
III.73-9   49
III.80   30

On the estate of Nikostratos
IV   4,39n.15,67,71,72,73,
             74,80,119
IV.2   119
IV.7   23n.32,23n.38,30
IV.8   119
IV.13   34n.5,67n.14
IV.14-5   62n.1
IV.15-7   75n.40
IV.18   76
IV.18-9   23n.32
IV.19   69n.22,70n.26,72,119
IV.24   119
IV.25   50n.62
IV.26   24n.40,69n.22,71n.32,
             72,119

On the estate of Dikaiogenes
V   4,39n.15,73,74,80,118
V.5   118
V.6   23n.32,24n.42,118
V.11   30
V.15-6   24n.42
V.16   40n.23,54n.73,118
V.16-7   118
V.36   30
V.47   39n.15

On the estate of Philoktemon
VI   4,26,28,39n.15,71,76,
             78
VI.3   40n.26,120
VI.3-5   120
VI.4   79n.44,120
VI.5   23n.37
VI.6   120
VI.7   23n.37
VI.9   23n.32
VI.9-10   62n.1
VI.10   120
VI.12-3   79n.44
VI.12-14   120
VI.15-6   24n.42
VI.17-22   5n.10
VI.19-26   79n.45
VI.21-6   122
VI.22-5   44n.43
VI.27   30
VI.28   84
VI.32   57n.76
VI.35-6   26n.54,26n.55
VI.36   122
VI.36-37   122
VI.37   122
VI.38   30n.69
VI.39-42   69n.22
VI.44   57,122
VI.44-5   122
VI.45   122
VI.63   56

On the estate of Apollodoros
VII   4,39n.16,53,56,62,74,
             76,117
VII.1   53n.71,62n.1,117
VII.1-2   67n.14
VII.1-3   117
VII.3   12
VII.5   117,119
VII.6   30,85
VII.7   22n.28,77,119
VII.9   20n.16, 22n.28,97,119
VII.14   21,23n.33,34
VII.15   34n.3
VII.15-7   36
VII.17   117
VII.18   117,124
VII.23   45n.46,124
VII.25   16,46n.47
VII.27   117
VII.27-8   54
VII.28   37
VII.29   77
VII.30   105,106
VII.30-2   68n.16,69n.21
VII.31   100,108,109n.5
VII.32   111
VII.34   22n.31
VII.44   109n.5

On the estate of Kiron
VIII   26,71,72,100,102
VIII.3   121
VIII.19   49n.58
VIII.21-7   69n.22,72
VIII.30-4   102,103
VIII.31   90n.3
VIII.31-3   72n.34
VIII.32   64n.3,65
VIII.34   40n.21
VIII.36   104n.24
VIII.38   71n.32
VIII.38-40   69n.22
VIII.39   72
VIII.40   26n.52,28n.61,101,121
VIII.40-2   5n.9,121
VIII.41   26n.51,121

On the estate of Astyphilos
IX   4,39n.15,67,71,72,73,
             74,80,120
IX.1   120
IX.2   24n.40,45n.46,120,123
IX.3   73n.38

IX.4	69n.22,70n.26, 73n.37,n.38	XI.45	20n.18,30,121
IX.6	120	XI.45-49	53n.70
IX.7	73n.38	XI.49	30,35n.8,44n.40,60n.91 100n.20,107n.4,123
IX.13	86n.59	XI.49-50	111,123
IX.14	120		
IX.15	23n.32	Frg.VIII	101n.22,121
IX.17	5n.9,120		
IX.18	120	Frg.IX	121
IX.27	120		
IX.32	69n.22,70n.26,73n.36	Frg. XXIV	90n.3
IX.33	45n.45,58n.78,123		
IX.36	120	ISOKRATES	
IX.37	62n.1	Aiginetikos	
		XIX	6

On the estate of Aristarchos

X	4,25n.45,39n.15,42, 60,73,74,80,99,101,119	LYKOURGOS *Against Leokrates*	
X.1-2	119	I.48	66n.11
X.2	43n.36,119	I.94	66n.7
X.3	119	I.147	70n.24
X.4	45n.45,124		
X.4-6	28n.62,119	LYSIAS	
X.5-6	99n.17,122	*On the murder of Eratosthenes*	
X.6	118,122	I.14	70n.26
X.7	124		
X.8	26n.50,43n.34,43n.37, 124	*Against Simon* III.3-4	5n.10
X.8-12	122		
X.9	38n.14,43n.37,84	*Against Agoratos*	
X.10	16	XIII.41	85
X.11	58n.78,59		
X.11-2	43n.37	*On the property of Aristophanes against the Treasury*	
X.12	90n.3		
X.13	95n.11	XIX.39-41	83
X.14	122		
X.14-5	43n.37	*Against Diogeiton*	
X.15	43n.34	XXXII.5-6	83
X.16	30	XXXII.11-3	5n.10
X.17	19,45n.45		
X.18-20	122	Frg.XXXI	97
X.19	94,99		
X.20	101n.21	Frg.LXXXVI	123
X.21	43n.34,122		
X.22	23n.32,119	MENANDER	
X.23	30	*Adelphoi II*	
		frg.6	66n.9

On the Estate of Hagnias

XI	73,107	Aspis	93
XI.8	23n.32,42n.32,79n.47, 120	258-69	93n.6
		270-73	102
XI.8-9	20n.17,57,120		
XI.9	120	*Dyskolos*	
XI.8-11	39n.17	738	96n.12
XI.11-3	2n.3,52n.68	748	96n.14
XI.41	20n.18,30		
XI.41-42	121		
XI.44	30		

Samia
10   38n.12
695-99   22

PAPYRI
P.Oxy.
XXXI.2538
  col.II,25-7   49n.58

PLUTARCH
Alkibiades
8.4   86n.58

[Lives of the Ten Orators]
834B   19
837C   30
838A   21n.21,117
838-9   118
839B   118

Moralia
843A   98n.16,125

Themistokles
32   98n.16,124

POLLUX
Onomastikon
VIII.39   31n.73,103n.23

THUKYDIDES
II.52   71n.31

XENOPHON
Memorabilia
II.2,13   70n.24

References to fragments of the Orators are to Baiter and Sauppe Oratores Attici *unless otherwise stated.*

General index

adoptees, age of 13,20,22
    rights of 26,27,51,56-7,58,61, 114
    obligations of 18n.8,57-61,114
adoption *inter vivos* 1,17,21-22,23,27,28,33,38,66,68,91,96-97,98
    and ἐμβάτευσις 40,45,47
    and γηροτροφία 13,66,78
    annulment of 18n.8,55-6
    contractual nature of 2,34-5,46-7, 54
ἀγχιστεία 2n.3,22,23-4,26,42,52,55, 99,101,105n.1
Archon, duties of 40,106,113
    and posthumous adoption 41,43, 55,105,113
archons, δοκιμασία of 75
ἀτιμία
    as punishment for adopting an ἄτιμος 19
    as punishment for maltreatment of parents 64
    incurred by public debtors 20,45, 60,101
ἄτιμος
    adoption of 19
    adoption of sons of 19-20,45
χάρις as constituent feature of father-son relationship 65-6,68,75
citizenship 6,9,18-9,48,66,84
civic identity 39n.15,48,55,66,75
commemorative rites (see tomb cult)
daughters
    and adopted sons 17,55-6,78,85, 87,95,96,97,99
    adoption of 1,20,57,87,89-90, 111
    rights of 25,27,87,95-6
daughters' sons
    adoption of,27-8,42,44,88-92,98, 99,104,111
    insecure position of 102,104
    rights of 28,44,79,87,90,96, 100-4,113
demes, enrolment in 2,6,26,33-5,37-38,44-5,46-8,50,53-5,57-58,59, 67-8,114
    corruption in 44
    membership of 18,20,48
Demotionidai, decrees of 36-7,49n.61
διαδικασία 2,73

διαμαρτυρία 12,31n.73,45,50n.63, 102-3
    by adopted sons 40,43,51,53,55
    on behalf of adopted sons 31n.73 40
    on behalf of daughters 78,91,102
    risk connected with 54,103
δίκη ψευδομαρτυρίων 27,40,43,50,54, 91,102
ἐγγύη 96,99-102,104
ἐμβάτευσις 18n.8,40,45,47,51,54,100 103
ἐπιδικασία 2,18n.8,25,26,28,39-40,41,43-4,45,50-5,79,87,91,92, 94,96,98,99,100,101,102,103, 107
    reopening of 18n.8,39n.16,41, 50,54-5,108-9,113
ἐπίκληρος 6,7,25-6,44,64,65,87-104, 105,106,111,113
    dissolution of marriage of 94, 98-100,103
family, changing concept of 5,7-9,12, 82,93-5,116
family-lines, continuation of 1,13-4,44, 60-1,68-9,75-6,77,78,82,86, 88-92,93,97,100,104,105,12
funeral 63,69,70-3,75
genos 11,68-9,71n.29
γηροτροφία 31,63,64-8,75,93
    and collateral relatives 64-8
γραφὴ κακώσεως γονέων 64
illegitimate children 79,92,102-3
intestate heirs 2n.3,63,77-81,93,115
    adoption of 24,27-8,44,78-80, 104,106,110,115
    obligations of 70-6,106-12
liturgists, liturgies 29-30,111-2
Menander 4-5,22,93,94,96
νομιζόμενα, τὰ 68,70,72,73
οἶκος concern of the entire community? 2-3,105-12,113,114
    continuation of, (see family-lines)
order of intestate succession 24-5,79, 87,114
    disruption of 25,63,76-81,110
παρακαταβολή 31n.73,39n.17,54,103
phratries, enrolment in 2,6,33-5,36-37,38-9,41-5,46-8,50,53-5, 57-8,59,67-8,114
    and daughters 49,91
    and minors 49
    obligatory membership of 19,49

πόλις
- disintegration of,7-9
- encouraging adoption? 2-3,105-9 113

posthumous adoption 1,8,13-4,25-,58-61,67,68,77,88-92,93,101,105-112,114
- and Archon 41,43,55,105-12,113
- of intestate heirs 2,27-8,44,73,75, 113
- procedure of 27-8,35,41-4,48,50, 55,107

Solon 10-2,17,58,71
- law on wills of 10-2,16-8,27,46, 62,76,81,83-4,112

testamentary adoption 1,12,13-4, 22-5,28,38,67,68,72,81-2,86,91, 96,98,110,114
- incomplete legal act?46-7
- unilateral nature of? 2,34-5, 46-7,54,86n.58

Thirty Tyrants 62,80,85

tomb cult 1,14-5,31,63,68,69-75,76,77,82,86,92,93,114
- obligations of collaterals 71, 73-6,109
- obligations of descendants 70, 72n.33

wills 8,22-5,27,76,78,80,89
- and legitimate sons 17,57,83-5
- revocation of 23,56-7
- sceptical attitude towards 12,74-5, 114
- without adoption 14,81-6,97,104, 114